THE PEOPLE OF THE SCOTTISH BURGHS

A Genealogical Source Book

The People of Arbroath
1600 - 1799

By David Dobson

CLEARFIELD

Copyright © 2014
by David Dobson
All Rights Reserved

Printed for Clearfield Company by
Genealogical Publishing Company
Baltimore, Maryland
2014

ISBN 978-0-8063-5704-1

INTRODUCTION

Arbroath lies on the east coast of Scotland and dates from 1178 when Arbroath Abbey was constructed by Tironsian monks. It was formerly known as Aberbrothock, meaning the settlement at the mouth of the Brothock river. The Scottish Declaration of Independence was subscribed by the king and nobles at the Abbey of Arbroath in 1320. Initially Arbroath was a Burgh of Regality under the rule of a representative of the king but by the mid sixteenth century it had become a Royal Burgh under the control of a council elected by the burgesses. Only the burgesses, who were craftsmen and merchants, had the right to vote, run businesses, etc. Many of them are included in this volume. As a Royal Burgh it was authorised to conduct overseas trade and had developed economic links with Scandinavia, the Baltic, the Netherlands, France, England and latterly America.

This book has been compiled as a source for genealogists and local historians wishing to identify primary source material pertaining to residents of Arbroath during the seventeenth and eighteenth centuries. The source citation given for each entry should be followed up and should provide useful data for those wishing to flesh out their family trees. The basic sources used by family historians and genealogists in Scotland are the Old Parish Registers of the Church of Scotland, which in the case of Arbroath begin in 1653. This source book, however, does provide much useful data, not covered by the OPRs, which should enable researchers to push the boundaries earlier than the limitations imposed by the church registers. Most of the entries are based on primary sources found in either the National Archives of Scotland or in Angus Archives, while Hay's 'History of Arbroath' has also proved useful. The burgh of Arbroath is spread over two parishes, Arbroath and St Vigeans, consequently data from both are included in this work together with some references from within five miles of the burgh boundary.

The People of Arbroath is designed as an aid to local historians and genealogists wishing to find information on inhabitants of Arbroath during the seventeenth and eighteenth centuries. It is based overwhelmingly on primary sources, such as the High Court of the Admiralty, the Commissary Courts, Customs and Excise Records, Exchequer Records, the Register of Deeds of the Court of Session, Burgh Records, Port Books, Services of Heirs, Register of Sasines, and monumental inscriptions, located in the National Archives of Scotland, Edinburgh, and the Angus Archives at Restenneth. It is not an exhaustive list of the inhabitants of Arbroath but rather an illustration of the records available. Each entry is fully referenced and should provide interesting material for those researching their family histories.

David Dobson, Dundee, 2014.

REFERENCES

AA	=	Angus Archives, Restenneth
ACB	=	Arbroath Court Book [ms]
AER	=	Examination Roll of Arbroath, 1752. [Edinburgh, 1987]
AJ	=	Aberdeen Journal, series
ASW	=	Aberdeen Shore Works Accounts, 1596-1670, [Aberdeen, 1972]
DLS	=	Directory of Landowning in Scotland, [Edinburgh, 1976]
F	=	Fasti Ecclesiae Scoticanae, [Edinburgh, 1920s]
HHA	=	History of Arbroath, [Arbroath, 1876]
JA	=	Jacobites of Angus 1689-1746, [Baltimore, 2002]
LC	=	Calendar of the Laing Charters, Edinburgh, 1899
MI	=	Monumental Inscription
NAS	=	National Archives of Scotland, Edinburgh
RGS	=	Register of the Great Seal of Scotland
RPCS	=	Register of the Privy Council of Scotland
SAB	=	Stads Arkivet, Bergen, Norway
SHS	=	Scottish History Society, Edinburgh
SIL	=	Letterbook of bailie John Steuart of Inverness, 1715-1752, [Edinburgh, 1915]
TNA	=	The National Archives, London

GLOSSARY

Baillie	=	burgh officer
Baxter	=	baker
Beadle	=	church officer
Box-master	=	treasurer
Brabiner	=	weaver
Chamberlain	=	manager
Comm.	=	commissariat
Cordiner	=	shoe-maker
Craft	=	trade
Currier	=	tanner
Deacon	=	chief official
Flax-dresser	=	one who prepares flax to spin into linen
Flesher	=	butcher
Freeman	=	a man free to trade within a burgh
Guilds-brother	=	a member of the merchant guild of a burgh
Hammerman	=	a metal worker
Hay-dresser	=	one who processes hay
Heckler	=	one who combs flax
Jacobite	=	a supporter of the House of Stuart
Land-waiter	=	a customs officer who taxes goods at a port
Litster	=	a dyer
Maltman	=	one who malts barley for brewing
Mr	=	a graduate, or son of a landed family
Provost	=	mayor
Reed-maker	=	one who makes reeds for music
Regality	=	a territory under the king's representative
Relict	=	widow
Sasine	=	a deed concerning property
Skinner	=	one who skins animals
Skipper	=	shipmaster
Stamp-master	=	quality controller of linen
Tide Surveyor	=	Customs officer who cargo loaded
Timberman	=	carpenter
Webster	=	weaver
White-ironsmith		maker of cast iron goods
Wright	=	wood or metal worker
Writer	=	lawyer

Arbroath Abbey

THE PEOPLE OF ARBROATH

1600-1799

ABBOT, JAMES, a dyer in Arbroath, a Jacobite in 1745. [JA]
ABERDEEN, ALEXANDER, deacon of the weavers craft of Arbroath, 1755. [AER.93]
ADAM, DAVID, in Auchenleck, burgess of Arbroath, 1685. [ACB][NAS.E69.11.1]; hearth tax, Arbroath,1691.
ADAM, GEORGE, in Cotton of East Seaton, husband of Janet Mannie who died 1744. [St Vigeans MI]
ADAM, GEORGE, town-clerk of Arbroath, 1716; testament, 1720, Comm. St Andrews. [NAS.AC13.1.163; RS35.XII.366/498]
ADAM, JOHN, 1664; servant to Alexander Hails in Arbroath, 1684. [NAS.GD45.16.1225] [AA.A1.14.60]
ADAM, JOHN, a shoemaker in Arbroath, 1737. [AER.94]
ADAM, MARGARET, daughter of John Adam, a wigmaker in Arbroath, 1750. [NAS.RS35.17.21]
ADAM, ROBERT, clerk of Arbroath, tenant of land in Punderlawfield, Arbroath, 1716. [NAS.E650/2]
ADAM, THOMAS, hearth tax, St Vigeans, 1691. [NAS.E69.11.1]
ADAM, WILLIAM, a weaver in Arbroath, 1740. [AER.93]
ADAMSON, JAMES, hearth tax, Arbroath, 1691. [NAS.E69.11.1]
ADAMSON, JOHN, hearth tax, St Vigeans, 1691. [NAS.E69.11.1]
ADAMSON, WILLIAM, hearth tax, St Vigeans, 1691. .138
ADDISON, ROBERT, a mariner in Arbroath, testament, 1776, Comm. St Andrews. [NAS]
AIKENHEAD, THOMAS, a skipper in Arbroath, testament, 1804, Comm. St Andrews. [NAS]
AIKMAN, ANDREW, a notary public in Arbroath, 1661. [RGS.XI.83]

AIKMAN, GEORGE, a councillor of Arbroath, 1617. [HHA. 150]

AIKMAN, ISOBEL, daughter of John Aikman the younger a burgess of Arbroath, heir to her grandfather John Aikman the elder a burgess of Arbroath, 1638. [NAS.Retours.Forfar]

AIKMAN, JOHN, a burgess of Arbroath in 1601, treasurer 1608, councillor 1617. [RGS.6.1197] [NAS.RS35.S2.1.90][HHA.138/146/150]

AIKMAN, JOHN, of Cairnie, St Vigeans, husband of Euphame Alexander, Crown charter, 1661. [RGS.XI.83]; Justice of the Peace of Arbroath, 1686; hearth tax, St Vigeans, 1691. [NAS.E69.11.1][RPCS.XI.574][RGS.XI.83]

AIKMAN, JOHN, a burgess of Arbroath, son of John Aikman and Janet Clark, father of Isabella and Nicola, sasine, 1638. [NAS.RS35.1.186; Retours.Forfar]

AIKMAN, JOHN, Provost of Arbroath, 1672, father of William Aikman an advocate. [HHA.156]

AIKMAN, JOHN, in Arbroath, 1699. [AA.A1.14.58]

AIKMAN, NICOLA, daughter of John Aikman the younger, a burgess of Arbroath, heir to her grand-father John Aikman the elder a burgess of Arbroath, 1638; in Arbroath, 1663. [NAS.Retours.Forfar][RGS.XI.444]

AIKMAN, THOMAS, a burgess of Arbroath, 1610. [RPCS. 8.727]

AIMAR, DAVID, hearth tax, Arbirlot, 1691. [NAS.E69.11.1]

AIMAR, GEORGE, hearth tax, Arbirlot, 1691. [NAS.E69.11.1]

AIMAR, JOHN, hearth tax, Arbirlot, 1691. [NAS.E69.11.1]

AIMAR, PATRICK, [1] hearth tax, Arbirlot, 1691. [NAS.E69.11.1]

AIMAR, PATRICK, [2], sr., hearth tax, Arbirlot, 1691. [NAS.E69.11.1]

AIMAR, PATRICK, [3], jr., hearth tax, Arbirlot, 1691. [NAS.E69.11.1]

AIRE, ALEXANDER, an officer of the shoe-maker craft in Arbroath, 1758. [AER.94]

AIR, DAVID, a flesher burgess, husband of Margaret Crawford, 1762. [Arbroath Abbey MI]

AIR, DAVID, a wright and militiaman, a burgess of Arbroath, 1797. [AA.18.941]

AIR, FRANCIS, a flesher in Arbroath, testament, 1744, Comm. St Andrews. [NAS]

AIRTH, ALEXANDER, in Arbirlot, 1691; born 1624, a smith in Bonniton, died 1693, father of Alexander Airth, born 1655, died 1707, grandfather of John, born 1692, died 1734. [NAS.E69.11.1][Arbirlot MI]

AIRTH, JOHN, hearth tax, St Vigeans, 1691. [NAS.E69.11.1]

AIRTH, JOHN, a wright burgess of Arbroath, 1797. [AA. 18.941]

AIRTH, WILLIAM, a shoe-maker in Arbroath, 1740, deacon of the craft, 1750s. [AER.94]

AITKIN, JOHN, born 1726, school-master of Arbroath in 1748, minister at St Vigeans from 1754 until 1816. [F. 5.450]

AITKENHEAD, DAVID, a mason in Arbroath, sasine,1760. [NAS.RS35.19.302; 20.399]

AITKENHEAD, THOMAS, born 1767, a skipper in Arbroath, died in Riga during 1804, husband of Elizabeth Dall. [Arbroath Abbey MI]

ALEXANDER, DAVID, a merchant in Arbroath, 1706. [NAS.CS229.C.1.73]

ALEXANDER, JAMES, a mariner in Arbroath, husband of Elspeth Edison, sasine,1735. [NAS.RS35.15.260; 22.33]

ALEXANDER, JOHN, master of the John and David of Arbroath, 1744-1745. [NAS.E504.1.1]

ALEXANDER, THOMAS, burgess of Arbroath, 1686. [ACB]

ALEXANDER, WILLIAM, a tailor in Arbroath, husband of Barbara Aikman, parents of Isabel Alexander, ca.1631. [NAS.RS35.S1.VIII.5]

ALEXANDER, WILLIAM, in Lochlands, Arbroath, 1658. [RGS.X.640]

ALLAN, ANDREW, servant to John Allan in Newton Arbirlot, testament, 1600, Comm. St Andrews. [NAS]

ALLAN, CHARLES, a merchant in Arbroath, sasine, 1779. [NAS.RS35.27.175]

ALLAN, JAMES, beadle of Arbroath, a Jacobite in 1715. [HHA.170][JA]

ALLAN, JOHN, in Newton Arbirlot, testament, 1605, Comm. St Andrews. [NAS]

ALLAN, GEORGE, a weaver burgess of Arbroath, 1797. [AA.18.941]

ALLAN, JAMES, a wright at Townhead of Arbroath, sasine, 1775. [NAS.RS35.25.341]

ALLAN, JOHN, a skinner burgess of Arbroath, 1610. [RPCS. 8.727]

ALLAN, JOHN, burgess of Arbroath, sasine,1656.
[NAS.RS35.S3.V.172]

ALLAN, THOMAS, burgess of Arbroath, 1610. [RPCS.8.727]

ALLAN, WILLIAM, born 1744, 'late of Jamaica', died 1818, husband of Mary Shanks, born 1768, died 1852.
[Arbroath Abbey MI]

ALLARDYCE, GEORGE, and spouse Margaret Alexander, in Arbroath, 1684; hearth tax, Arbroath, 1691.
[AA.A1.14.104][NAS.E69.11.1]

ALLARDYCE, JAMES, a notary public in Arbroath, 1681.
[ACB][HHA.157]

ALLARDYCE, JOHN, Provost of Arbroath, and his relict Anne Philp, sasine,1768. [NAS.RS35.22.392, etc]

AMBROSE, DAVID, born 1734, died 1 June 1799, deacon of the weavers of Arbroath 1768, husband of Elizabeth Scott. [Arbroath Abbey MI][AER.93]

AMBROSE, JOHN, deacon of the weavers in Arbroath, 1752.
[AER.93]

ANDERSON, ALEXANDER, born 1604, in Easter Inverpeffer, died 1648, husband of Elspet Anderson, born 1606, died 1679. [Arbirlot MI]

ANDERSON, ALEXANDER, burgess of Arbroath, sasine, 1653. [NAS.RS35.S2.IV.191]

ANDERSON, ALEXANDER, burgess of Arbroath, 1692.
[ACB]

ANDERSON, ALEXANDER, hearth tax, Arbroath, 1691.
[NAS.E69.11.1]

ANDERSON, ALEXANDER, hearth tax, Arbirlot, 1691.
[NAS.E69.11.1]

ANDERSON, ALEXANDER, a weaver in Arbroath, 1764.
[AER.93]

ANDERSON, DAVID, hearth tax, St Vigeans, 1691.
[NAS.E69.11.1]

ANDERSON, HECTOR, burgess of Arbroath, spouse Katherine Durward, sasine, 1640; 1664.
[NAS.RS35.S2.1.379; GD45.16.1225]

ANDERSON, HENDRY, born 1724, tenant in Greenford, died 1794, spouse Elisabeth Sutter. [Arbirlot MI]

ANDERSON, HENRY, by the Brothock Water, Arbroath, a merchant burgess of Arbroath, son of James Anderson, sasine and deeds,1653;1658; 1659; 1661. [RGS.X.640]
[NAS.RD3.3.87; RD2.1.393; RS35.S2.1.66]

ANDERSON, JAMES, merchant burgess of Arbroath, 1684; hearth tax, Arbroath, 1691; 1699. [ACB][AA.A1.14.92] [NAS.E69,11.1]

ANDERSON, JAMES, hearth tax, St Vigeans, 1691. [NAS.E69.11.1]

ANDERSON, JAMES, from Aberdeen, a burgess of Arbroath, 1696. [ACB]

ANDERSON, JAMES, a merchant in Arbroath, testament, 1726, Comm. St Andrews. [NAS]

ANDERSON, JAMES, in Wormyhills, Arbirlot, 1799. [NAS.GD45.18.2012]

ANDERSON, JOHN, in Arbroath, 1664. [NAS.GD45.16.1225]

ANDERSON, JOHN, hearth tax, Arbirlot, 1691. [NAS.E69.11.1]

ANDERSON, Mrs, widow of John Anderson, hearth tax, Arbroath, 1691. [NAS.E69.11.1]

ANDERSON, JOHN, hearth tax, St Vigeans, 1691. [NAS.E69.11.1]

ANDERSON, JOHN, a burgess of Arbroath, hearth tax, 1691; a tailor in Arbroath, a deed, 1699. [ACB][NAS.E69.11.1; RD4.84.995]

ANDERSON, JOHN, tenant of land in Keptie and Dishland, Arbroath 1716. [NAS.E650/2]

ANDERSON, JOHN, a tailor in Arbroath, son of ... Anderson and his wife Isobel Alexander, husband of Isobel Duncan, sasine, 1703. [NAS.RS35.10.318, etc]

ANDERSON, JOHN, in Millgait, Arbroath, 1724. [NAS.GD3.14.2.1.44]

ANDERSON, WILLIAM, a tailor in Arbroath, husband of Jean Strachan, sasine,1645. [NAS.RS35.S2.II.438]

ANDERSON, WILLIAM, a sailor from Arbroath, died on the St Andrew at Darien in 1698, testament, 1707, Comm. Edinburgh. [NAS]

ANDERSON, WILLIAM, a merchant in Arbroath, 1749. [NAS.AC9.1661]

ANDERSON, WILLIAM, brother of John Anderson, a tailor in Arbroath, sasine,1751. [NAS.RS35.17.299]

ANDERSON, WILLIAM, a shoemaker in Arbroath, 1767. [AER.94]

ANDERSON, WILLIAM, a manufacturer in Arbroath, testament, 1785, Comm. St Andrews. [NAS]

ANDREW, ALEXANDER, a merchant in Arbroath, 1733. [AER.95]

ANITH, ISABEL, hearth tax, Arbroath, 1691. [NAS.E69.11.1]

ANNANDALE, JOHN, born 1720 son of John Annandale and his wife Helen Arnold, a shoemaker in Arbroath, a Jacobite in 1745. [JA][AER.94]

ANTON, WILLIAM, a writer from Edinburgh, burgess of Arbroath, 1698. [ACB]

ARCHER, WILLIAM, a tailor in Arbroath, a Jacobite in 1745. [JA]

ARNOTT, ALEXANDER, hearth tax, St Vigeans, 1691. [NAS.E69.11.1]

ARNOTT, DAVID, hearth tax, St Vigeans, 1691. [NAS.E69.11.1]

ARNOTT, JAMES, son of David Arnott, a burgess of Arbroath, 1692. [ACB]

ARNOT, JAMES, born 1733, a weaver 1765, died 1783, husband of Margaret Dall, born 1730, died 1813. [Arbroath Abbey MI][AER.93]

ARRAT, THOMAS, a merchant in Arbroath, sasine,1752, 1758. [NAS.RS35.17.541; E326.1.133]

AUCHINLECK, ..., an Episcopal preacher and a Jacobite in Arbirlot, 1715. [HHA.170]

AUCHTERLONIE, ALEXANDER, son of William Auchterlonie of Auchterlonie, burgess of Arbroath, 1609. [RGS.7.90]

AUCHTERLONIE, ALEXANDER, [1], hearth tax, Arbirlot, 1691. [NAS.E69.11.1]

AUCHTERLONIE, ALEXANDER, [2], hearth tax, Arbirlot, 1691. [NAS.E69.11.1]

AUCHTERLONIE, ALEXANDER, burgess of Arbroath, 1683; hearth tax, Arbroath, 1691. [ACB][NAS.E69.11.1]

AUCHTERLONIE, ALEXANDER, a merchant in Arbroath, testament, 1722, Comm. St Andrews. [NAS]

AUCHTERLONY, ALEXANDER, son of George Auchterlonie, late Provost of Arbroath, and Agnes Wallace, daughter of William Wallace late baillie there, an antenuptial marriage contract, 22 December 1747; a writer and bailie of Arbroath and co-owner of the St Thomas of Arbroath, 1743, husband of Agnes Wallace, sasine. [NAS.GD243.21.3/11;AC9.1500; RS35.17.242, etc; E326.1.133]

AUCHTERLONIE, ANDREW, burgess of Arbroath, 1592; 1601. [HHA.138/145]
AUCHTERLONIE, ANDREW, burgess of Arbroath, a sasine, 1652. [NAS.RS35.S2.IV.174]
AUCHTERLONIE, DAVID, commissioner for Arbroath, 1606. [HHA.139]
AUCHTERLONIE, DAVID, a maltman in Arbroath, 1606. [HHA.144]
AUCHTERLONIE, DAVID, a councillor of Arbroath in 1657 and a bailie there, sasine, 1661. [NAS.RS3.3.201]
AUCHTERLONIE, DAVID hearth tax, Arbirlot, 1691. [NAS.E69.11.1]
AUCHTERLONIE, GEORGE, son of John Auchterlonie of Guynd, burgess of Arbroath, 1688. [ACB]
AUCHTERLONIE, HELEN, relict of Sir Patrick Wallace, in Arbroath, 1725. [NAS.GD3.14.2.1.54]
AUCHTERLONIE, JAMES, of Seaton, 1599. [LC.1387]
AUCHTERLONIE, JAMES, son of Patrick Ogilvie, a burgess of Arbroath, a sasine, 1676. [NAS.RS35.S3.VI.81]
AUCHTERLONIE, JAMES, hearth tax, Arbroath, 1691. [NAS.E69.11.1]
AUCHTERLONY, JAMES, a merchant in Arbroath, 1737. [NAS.AC8.549]
AUCHTERLONIE, JOHN, commissioner of Arbroath, 1617. [HHA.150]
AUCHTERLONIE, JOHN, Provost of Arbroath 1653, councillor there 1655-1657. [NAS.AC2.1][HHA.156]
AUCHTERLONIE, JOHN, of Guynd, hearth tax, Arbroath, 1691. [NAS.E69.11.1]
AUCHTERLONIE, JOHN, hearth tax, Arbroath, 1691. [NAS.E69.11.1]
AUCHTERLONIE, PATRICK, son of John Auchterlonie of Guynd, a cordiner burgess of Arbroath, a sasine, 1643. [NAS.RS35.S2.II.104]
AUCHTERLONIE, PATRICK, a burgess of Arbroath, a sasine, 1675; hearth tax, Arbroath, 1691. [NAS.RS35.S2.II.104; E69.11.1]
AUCHTERLONY, PATRICK, master of the 75 ton Clementina of Arbroath, 1726, Gloucester of Arbroath, 1736, of the Goodwill of Arbroath, 1740, and the Friendship of Arbroath, 1744. [NAS.CE53.1.2/3; AC11/158B]

AUCHTERLONIE, ROBERT, a councillor of Arbroath, 1617. [HHA.150]

AUCHTERLONY, ROBERT, a skipper in Arbroath, master of the Concord of Arbroath, 1716. [NAS.AC9.585; AC13/1/163]

AUCHTERLONIE, WILLIAM, a burgess of Arbroath, 1606. [ACB][HHA.143]

AUCHTERLONIE, WILLIAM, and his spouse Margaret Lindsay, a sasine, Arbroath, 1642. [NAS.RS35.S2.II.106]

AUCHTERLONIE, WILLIAM, a councillor in 1681, a baillie in 1691, hearth tax, Arbroath, 1691. [NAS.E69.11.1][RPCS.XVI.705][HHA.157]

BADIE, JOHN, a seaman in Auchmithie by Arbroath, testament, 1606, St Andrews. [NAS]

BALBIRNIE, JAMES, a burgess of Arbroath, 1692. [ACB]

BALFOUR, DAVID, a burgess of Arbroath, husband of Jane Rossie, testament, 1608, Comm. of Edinburgh. [NAS]

BALFOUR, PATRICK, a baillie burgess of Arbroath, 1601. [RGS.VI.1155]

BALNEAVES, HENRY, a burgess of Arbroath, 1687. [ACB]

BANNERMAN, WILLIAM, hearth tax, St Vigeans, 1691. [NAS.E69.11.1]

BANNERMAN, JOHN, a weaver in Arbroath, 1764. [AER.93]

BARCLAY, DAVID, born 1720, son of James Barclay and his wife Isabel Butchart, a brewer in Arbroath, a Jacobite in 1745. [JA]

BARCLAY, Miss MOLLY, in Almerie Close, Arbroath, 1752. [AER]

BARCLAY, ROBERT, in Arbroath, 1753. [NAS.E326.1.133]

BARCLAY, ROBERT ALLARDYCE, of Urie, a burgess of Arbroath, 1789. [AA.18.941]

BARCLAY, Miss WILLIAMINA, in Almerie Close, Arbroath, 1752. [AER]

BARRIE, GEORGE, a weaver burgess of Arbroath, 1789. [AA.18.941]

BARRIE, JOHN, in Arbroath, 1658. [RGS.X.640]

BARRIE, JOHN, hearth tax, Arbroath, 1691. [NAS.E69.11.1]

BARRIE, WILLIAM, a mason in Arbroath, sasine, 1765. [NAS.RS35.20.353/412]

BARKER, JAMES, a weaver burgess of Arbroath, 1797, [AA.18.941]

BAULD, ANDREW, a merchant in Arbroath, 1796.
[NAS.CS230.SEQN.B.1.15]
BAXTER, ANDREW, a burgess of Arbroath, 1692. [ACB]
BAXTER, JAMES, a burgess of Arbroath, a sasine,1631.
[NAS.RS35.S1.VIII.161]
BEAT, ALEXANDER, a merchant in Arbroath, husband of Margaret Mitchell, testament, 1775, Comm. St Andrews. [NAS]
BEATON, DAVID, feuar of Carsegownie, a burgess of Arbroath, 1601. [ACB]
BEATTIE, WILLIAM, born 1773, a skipper in Arbroath, died 1816. [Arbroath Abbey MI]
BELL, JAMES, a merchant in Arbroath, a trustee, 1791.
[NAS.CS96.2037]
BELL, ROBERT, a merchant from Dundee, admitted as a burgess of Arbroath 1748. [NAS.GD1.449.378]
BELL, Reverend WILLIAM, born 1720, educated at Marischal College, Aberdeen, minister at Arbroath from 1743 until 1775, husband of Bethia Willison, parents of James, Margaret, and Isabella; 1753. [NAS.E326.1.133] [F.5.424]
BENNETT, JAMES, a burgess of Arbroath, 1685; hearth tax, Arbroath, 1691. [ACB][NAS.E69.11.1]
BENNETT, WILLIAM, hearth tax, St Vigeans, 1691.
[NAS.E69.11.1]
BELL, WILLIAM, born 1720, educated at Marischal College, minister at Arbroath from 1748 until 1775, husband of Behia Willison, parents of James, Margaret, and Isabella.
[F.5.424]
BERTIE, JOHN, servant to Sir John Carnegie of Southesk, a burgess of Arbroath, 1789. [AA.18.941]
BIZET, GEORGE, master of the Jean of Arbroath, trading with Scandinavia,1740s. [NAS.E504.24.1/2]
BLACK, ALEXANDER, hearth tax, Arbroath, 1691.
[NAS.E69.11.1]
BLACK, ALEXANDER, a weaver burgess, born 1685, died 1747, husband of Helen Hunter. [Arbroath Abbey MI]
BLACK, DAVID, educated at St Andrews, minister of Arbirlot, 1597 until his death in 1603, husband of Katherine Prattie, parents of Sarah. [F.5.420]
BLACK, HENRY, born 1627, deacon of the weavers of Arbroath, a burgess of Arbroath, hearth tax, 1691, died 1707. [Arbroath Abbey MI] [NAS.E69.11.1]

BLACK, JAMES, a burgess of Arbroath, son of Alexander Black a weaver, sasine 1762. [AA.A1.14.130]

BLACK, JOHN, a merchant burgess of Arbroath, 1798. [AA.18.941]

BLAIR, Sir ALEXANDER, of Balthyock, a burgess of Arbroath, 1687. [ACB]

BLAIR, DAVID, from Bo'ness, a burgess of Arbroath, 1682. [ACB]

BLAIR, GEORGE, a cornet of Lord Carmichael's troop of Dragoons, a burgess of Arbroath, 1695. [ACB]

BLAIR, JOHN, of Pokmilne, a burgess of Arbroath, 1687. [ACB]

BOATH, JAMES, a weaver burgess of Arbroath, 1797, [AA.18.941]

BOATH, JOHN, a weaver burgess of Arbroath, 1797. [AA.18.941]

BODIE, DAVID, hearth tax, St Vigeans, 1691. [NAS.E69.11.1]

BODDIE, JOHN, a fisherman in Auchmithie, 1732. [NAS.GD130]

BOOTH, WILLIAM, a burgess of Arbroath, 1690. [ACB]

BOSWELL, ROBERT, a burgess of Arbroath, 1795. [AA.18.941]

BOUMAN, AGNES, hearth tax, Arbroath, 1691. [NAS.E69.11.1]

BOWDEN, JOHN, deacon of the hammermen of Arbroath, 1680. [HHA.289]

BOWER, GEORGE, a weaver in Arbroath, 1742, deacon of the weaver craft 1750. [AER.93]

BOWICK, THOMAS, a mason in Arbroath, spouse Isobel Philip, sasine, 1772. [NAS.RS35.23.432]

BOYACK, THOMAS, a mason in Arbroath, husband of Isobel Philip, sasine, 1718. [NAS.RS35.13.430]

BOYDAN, JOHN, hearth tax, Arbroath, 1691. [NAS.E69.11.1]

BRAND, ALEXANDER, in London, a burgess of Arbroath, 1790. [AA.18.941]

BRAND, JAMES, in London, a burgess of Arbroath, 1790. [AA.18.941]

BREMNER, JOHN, a weaver burgess of Arbroath, 1797. [AA.18.941]

BROCKES, GEORGE, schoolmaster at St Vigeans, 1690; a Jacobite in 1715. [SHS.4.2][HHA.170]

BRODIE, GEORGE, a writer burgess of Arbroath, 1797.
[AA.18.941]
BROWN, AGNES, died 1647. [Arbroath Abbey MI]
BROWN, ALEXANDER, hearth tax, Arbroath, 1691.
[NAS.E69.11.1]
BROWN, ALEXANDER, hearth tax, Arbirlot, 1691.
[NAS.E69.11.1]
BROWN, ALEXANDER, a weaver burgess of Arbroath 1797.
[AA.18.941]
BROWN, CHRISTIAN, in Arbroath, testament, 1777,
Comm. St Andrews. [NAS]
BROWN, DAVID, a weaver burgess of Arbroath 1797. [AA.
18.941]
BROUN, GEORGE, hearth tax, St Vigeans, 1691.
[NAS.E69.11.1]
BROWN, JAMES, a shoemaker in Arbroath, 1737. [AER.94]
BROWN, WILLIAM, in Lochlands, a burgess of Arbroath,
husband of Margaret Murtone, a sasine, 1652; 1658;
1663. [RGS.X.640; XI.444] [NAS.RS35.S2.IV.191]
BROWN, WILLIAM, of Gladsmuir, a resident in Arbroath,
testaments, 1767, 1782, Comm. St Andrews. [NAS]
[NAS.RS35.25.344]
BROWN, WILLIAM, born 1734, a saddle-maker, died 1775,
husband of Isabel Mudie. [Arbroath Abbey MI]
BROWN, WILLIAM, a shoemaker in Arbroath, 1770. [AER.
94]
BRUCE, Sir ALEXANDER, of Broomhall, a burgess of
Arbroath, 1694. [ACB]
BRUCE, Mr DAVID, a burgess of Arbroath, 1696. [ACB]
BRUCE, JAMES, in Muirden, Arbroath, 1752. [AER]
BRUCE, JOHN, of Muirden, a vintner in Arbroath, 1768.
[NAS.GD45.12.144]
BRUCE, JON., in Almerie Close, Arbroath, 1752. [AER]
BRUCE, Mr THOMAS, the General Muster Master, a burgess
of Arbroath, 1694. [ACB]
BRUCE, THOMAS, the Commissary General, burgess of
Arbroath, 1694. [ACB]
BRUCE, WILLIAM, in Arbroath, 1753. [NAS.E326.1.133]
BRUCE, WILLIAM, a skipper in Arbroath, testament, Comm.
St Andrews. [NAS]
BUCHAN, COLIN, in Almerie Close, Arbroath, 1752. [AER]
BUCHAN, WILLIAM, a burgess of Arbroath, 1627.
[RPCS.II.23]

BULL, CATHERINE, hearth tax, St Vigeans, 1691.
[NAS.E69.11.1]
BURN, Captain JOHN, in Arbroath, 1753. [NAS.E326.1.133]
BURN, JOHN, minister at St Vigeans from 1731 until 1734.
[F.5.450]
BURNESS, JAMES, a writer in Montrose, a burgess of
Arbroath, 1789. [AA.18.941]
BURNET, JAMES, a merchant burgess of Arbroath, 1794.
[AA.18.941]; born 1770, died 28 May 1807, husband of
Jean Strachan. [Arbroath Abbey MI]
BURNS, JAMES, a carter burgess of Arbroath, 1797. [AA.
18.941]
BURNS, ROBERT, hearth tax, Arbirlot, 1691.
[NAS.E69.11.1]
BURNS, WILLIAM, a carter burgess of Arbroath, 1797. [AA.
18.941]
BUTCHART, ALEXANDER, a manufacturer burgess of
Arbroath, 1797. [AA.18.941]
BUTCHART, ANN, in Hercules Den, Arbroath, 1752. [AER]
BUTCHARD, DAVID, hearth tax, Arbirlot, 1691.
[NAS.E69.11.1]
BUTCHART, JAMES, master of the Elizabeth of Arbroath
trading with Holland, 1682. [NAS.E72.7.9]
BUTCHART, JAMES, a merchant bailie of Arbroath, husband
of Elizabeth Dais, 1748. [Arbroath Abbey MI]
[NAS.E326.1.133]; in Berryfauld, Arbroath, 1752.
[AER]; 1768.[NAS.GD45.12.194]
BUTCHER, JOHN, in Arbroath, 1658/1667. [RGS.X.640; XI.444]
BUTCHARD, JOHN, hearth tax, Arbirlot, 1691.
[NAS.E69.11.1]
BUTCHART, JON., in Gallowden, Arbroath, 1752. [AER]
BUTCHART, ROBERT, a manufacturer burgess of Arbroath,
1797. [AA.18.941]
BUTCHARD, THOMAS, hearth tax, St Vigeans, 1691.
[NAS.E69.11.1]
BUTCHART, WILLIAM, a manufacturer burgess of
Arbroath, 1797. [AA.18.941]
CAIRD, ANDREW, hearth tax, Arbirlot, 1691.
[NAS.E69.11.1]
CAIRD, DAVID, a burgess of Arbroath, 1789. [AA.18.941]
CAIRD, JAMES, a weaver burgess of Arbroath, 1797; relict
Jean Campbell, testament, 1799, Comm. St Andrews.
[NAS] [AA.18.941]

CAIRD, JOHN, a confectioner burgess of Arbroath, 1793. [AA.18.941]
CAIRY, DAVID, a burgess of Arbroath, 1795. [AA.18.941]
CALLANDER, ALEXANDER, in Creighton, a burgess of Arbroath, 1789. [AA.18.941]
CAMPBELL, JOHN, hearth tax, St Vigeans, 1691. [NAS.E69.11.1]
CAMPBELL, WILLIAM, hearth tax, Arbroath, 1691. [NAS.E69.11.1]
CANT, JAMES, a baker burgess of Arbroath, 1795. [AA.18.941]
CANT, THOMAS, a cabinet-maker burgess of Arbroath, 1797. [AA.18.941]
CARGILL, DAVID, a burgess of Arbroath, 1696. [ACB]
CARGILL, DAVID, a skipper in Auchmithie by Arbroath, husband of Grizel, parents of Catherine, John and Robert, sasine, ca.1670. [NAS.RS35.s3.4.296, etc]
CARGILL, DAVID, a fisherman in Auchmithie, probably a smuggler in 1768. [NAS.CE53.1.5]
CARGILL, DAVID, a landowner in 1770. [DLS.26]
CARGILL, DAVID, master of the Bell and Ann of Arbroath, 1798. [AJ.2617]
CARGILL, DAVID LAWSON, born 1781, a skipper in Arbroath, died 1819. [Arbroath Abbey MI]
CARGILL, HELEN, hearth tax, St Vigeans, 1691. [NAS.E69.11.1]
CARGILL, JAMES, hearth tax, St Vigeans, 1691. [NAS.E69.11.1]
CARGILL, JAMES, born 16..., skipper in Auchmithie, husband of Katherine, died 17... [St Vigean's MI]; fisherman in Auchmithie, 1732. [NAS.GD130]
CARGILL, JOHN, son of David Cargill, a skipper in Auchmithie, sasine, ca.1690. [NAS.RS35.s3.8.59]
CARGILL, JOHN, sr. and jr., hearth tax, St Vigeans, 1691. [NAS.E69.11.1]
CARGILL, JOHN, born 1704, a skipper in Auchmithie, died in Arbroath 1771. [St Vigeans MI]; master of the Alexander of Auchmithie, 1744. [NAS.E504.24.1]
CARGILL, JOHN, born 1765, a skipper burgess of Arbroath, 1796, died 1843, husband of Ann Paterson. [AA.18.941] [Arbroath Abbey MI]
CARGILL, ROBERT, son of David Cargill, a skipper in Auchmithie, sasine, ca.1690. [NAS.RS35.s3.8.59]

CARGILL, ROBERT, a burgess of Arbroath, 1698. [ACB]

CARGILL, ROBERT, sr., a fisherman in Auchmithie, 1732. [NAS.GD130]

CARGILL, ROBERT, jr., a fisherman in Auchmithie, 1732. [NAS.GD130]

CARGILL, ROBERT, born 1734, a skipper in Arbroath, master of the Robert and Jean of Arbroath, and his son Robert, were shipwrecked and drowned off Macduff in 1787, husband of Jean Lawson. [Arbroath Abbey MI] [Banff MI][AJ.2050]

CARGILL, THOMAS, a baker burgess of Arbroath, 1799. [AA.18.941]

CARGILL, WILLIAM, a fisherman in Auchmithie, 1732. [NAS.GD130]

CARGILL, WILLIAM, master of the Happy Return of Auchmithie, 1740s. [NAS.E504.24.1]

CARMICHAEL, JOHN, a servant of the Earl of Panmure, a burgess of Arbroath, 1696. [ACB]

CARMICHAEL, JOHN, a skipper, died 1735, testament, 1735, Comm. St Andrews. [NAS][Arbroath Abbey MI]

CARMICHAEL, THOMAS, late baillie to Montrose, hearth tax, Arbroath, 1691. [NAS.E69.11.1]

CARNEGY, ALEXANDER, the Sheriff Depute of Forfar, a burgess of Arbroath, 1683. [ACB]

CARNEGIE, ALEXANDER, born in Arbroath 1705, son of Robert Carnegie and his wife Janet Blair, a Jacobite transported to Maryland in 1747. [JA][TNA.T1.328]

CARNEGIE, DAVID, Earl of Southesk, a burgess of Arbroath, 1693. [ACB]

CARNEGIE, GEORGE, a burgess of Arbroath, 1793. [AA. 18.941]

CARNEGIE, JAMES, born 1633, son of Alexander Carnegie of Cookston, graduated MA from the University of St Andrews in 1653, minister of Arbroath from 1669 to his death in 1686, husband of Isobel Hay, parents of Alexander and Anna. [F.5.424]

CARNEGIE, JAMES, of Newgait, Justice of the Peace of Arbroath, 1686. [RPCS.XI.574]

CARNEGIE, JAMES, hearth tax, St Vigeans, 1691. [NAS.E69.11.1]

CARNEGIE, Sir JAMES, of Pitarrow, a burgess of Arbroath, 1687. [ACB]

CARNEGIE, JAMES, a merchant in Arbroath, 1729. [NAS.AC9.1083]

CARNEGIE, JOHN, Arbroath, 1691. [NAS.E69.11.1]

CARNEGIE, JOHN, master of the Grammar School of Arbroath, burgess of Arbroath, 1690, husband of Grisell West, died 1699. [Arbroath Abbey MI]

CARNEGIE, Reverend JOHN, in Inverkeilor, a burgess of Arbroath, 1791. [AA.18.941]

CARNEGIE, PATRICK, chamberlain of Arbroath in 1613, and a bailie there in 1617. [NAS.GD3.2.24.13][HHA. 149]

CARNEGIE, PATRICK, a burgess of Arbroath, husband of Catherine Hailes, a sasine 1637. [NAS.RS35.S2.1.24]

CARNEGIE, Mr PATRICK, brother of the Earl of Northesk, a burgess of Arbroath, 1683; a Justice of the Peace of Arbroath, 1686.[RPCS.XI.574] [ACB]

CARNEGY, ROBERT, of Newgait, Arbroath, tenant of Punderlawfield, Arbroath, 1716. [NAS.E650/2]

CARNEGIE, WILLIAM, son of Alexander Carnegie of Crookston, graduated MA from the University of St Andrews in 1667, minister of Arbroath from 1686 until his death in 1694, husband of Jean Carnegie, parents of Charles Carnegie; testament, 1708, Comm. Brechin. [NAS][F.5.424]

CARNEGIE, WILLIAM, a weaver in Arbroath, 1737. [AER. 93]

CARRIE, DAVID, born 1738, died 1792. [Arbroath Abbey MI]

CARRIE, JOHN, a pedlar in Arbroath, a Jacobite in1745, transported to Maryland in 1747. [JA][TNA.T1.28]

CARSWELL, JOHN, a litster burgess, born 1686, died 29 February 1741, husband of Margaret Cant. [Arbroath Abbey MI]

CASSELS, JOHN, hearth tax, Arbroath, 1691. [NAS.E69.11.1]

CASWELL, JOHN, a litster in Arbroath, 1737, 1738. [NAS.AC8/549, 565]

CATHRO, WILLIAM, hearth tax, Arbirlot, 1691. [NAS.E69.11.1]

CATHROW, WILLIAM, a brewer burgess of Arbroath, 1792. [AA.18.941]

CHAIKARD, DAVID, a burgess of Arbroath, testament, 1614, Comm. St Andrews. [NAS]

CHALMERS, ALEXANDER, a shoe-maker burgess of Arbroath, 1797. [AA.18.941]

CHALMERS, JAMES, late brewer in Arbroath, relict Katherine Forsyth, testament, 1767, Comm. St Andrews. [NAS]

CHALMERS, JOHN, in Drunkendub, St Vigeans, a Jacobite in 1745. [JA]

CHAMBER, CORNELIUS, hearth tax, Arbroath, 1691. [NAS.E69.11.1]

CHAMBERS, PATRICK, hearth tax, St Vigeans, 1691. [NAS.E69.11.1]

CHAPEL, DAVID, a weaver in Arbroath, 1759. [AER.93]

CHAPEL, JOHN, a butcher burgess of Arbroath, 1799. [AA.18.941]

CHAPEL, JOHN, born 1745, ship-owner in Arbroath, died 1817, husband of Katherine Smith, born 1748, died 1813. [Arbroath Abbey MI]

CHAPEL, WILLIAM, a weaver burgess of Arbroath, 1797. [AA.18.941]

CHAPLAIN, JEAN, a mantua maker in Arbroath, daughter of the late James Chaplain of Colliston, and her husband William Jamieson, a barber in Montrose, who married in December 1761, Process of Adherence, 5 June 1771, and Process of Divorce on 18 June 1773, Commissariat of Edinburgh. [NAS]

CHAPLINE, Reverend ALEXANDER, in Kinnell, a burgess of Arbroath, 1791. [AA.18.941]

CHAPLIN, ...landowner of Colliston, 1770. [DLS.26]

CHARTERIS, CHARLES, born in East Lothian 1673, graduated MA Edinburgh in 1697, minister at Arbirlot from 1702 until 1729, husband of Marjory Williamson, parents of Marjory. [F.5.421]

CHERITT, PETER, hearth tax, St Vigeans, 1691. [NAS.E69.11.1]

CHEVIS, JAMES, a bailie of Arbroath, husband of Elspeth Mackie, sasine, 1704. [NAS.RS35.11.202]

CHIVAS, JAMES, hearth tax, Arbroath, 1691. [NAS.E69.11.1]

CHISHOLM, ALEXANDER, a wright burgess of Arbroath, 1797. [AA.18.941]

CHRYSTIE, ALEXANDER, hearth tax, Arbroath, 1691. [NAS.E69.11.1]

CHRISTIE, DAVID, a tailor burgess of Arbroath, testament, 1681, Comm. St Andrews. [NAS]
CHRISTIE, DAVID, in the Brow of Milton, a burgess of Arbroath, 1695. [ACB]
CHRISTIE, GEORGE, a merchant burgess of Arbroath, 1795. [AA.18.941]
CHRISTIE, JAMES, in Arbroath, 1658/1663; testament, 1673, Comm. St Andrews. [NAS][RGS.X.640; XI.444]
CHRISTIE, JAMES, a mariner in Arbroath, testament, 1685, Comm. St Andrews. [NAS]
CHRISTIE, JAMES, hearth tax, Arbroath, 1691; burgess of Arbroath, 1693. [NAS.E69.11.1][ACB]
CHRISTIE, JAMES, a skipper of Arbroath, 1704, 1705. [NAS.AC8.23; AC9.166]
CHRISTIE, JAMES, a shoe-maker in Arbroath, 1746. [AER. 94]
CHRISTIE, JAMES, a burgess of Arbroath, 1799. [AA. 18.941]
CHRISTIE, KATHERINE, in Muirden, Arbroath, 1752. [AER]
CHRISTY, WILLIAM, a mason burgess of Arbroath, 1797. [AA.18.941]
CHRISTIE, ..., master of the Royal Ann of Arbroath, 1752. [AJ.257]
CLARK, ALEXANDER, hearth tax, St Vigeans, 1691. [NAS.E69.11.1]
CLARK, ANDREW, a burgess of Arbroath, 1688. [ACB]
CLARK, DAVID, master of the John and David of Arbroath, 1745. [NAS.E504.1.1/2]
CLERK, JAMES, hearth tax, St Vigeans, 1691. [NAS.E69.11.1]
CLARK, JAMES, a baker burgess of Arbroath, 1794. [AA. 18.941]
CLARK, JOHN, a merchant burgess of Arbroath, 1794. [AA. 18.941]
CLARK, THOMAS, hearth tax, St Vigeans, 1691. [NAS.E69.11.1]
CLAYSON, EDWARD, of the frigate Champion, a burgess of Arbroath, 1790. [AA.18.941]
CLEATON, DAVID, a weaver in Arbroath, 1737. [AER.93]
COCKBURN, ANDREW, a litster burgess of Arbroath, testament, 1618, Comm. St Andrews. [NAS]
COB, WILLIAM, a weaver in Arbroath, 1764. [AER.93]

COCKBURN, Sir WILLIAM, a burgess of Arbroath, 1795. [AA.18.941]

COLLENG, Captain SAMUEL, a burgess of Arbroath, 1797. [AA.18.941]

COLLIE, WILLIAM, son of William Collie a burgess of Arbroath and his wife Marjory Futhie, settled in Denmark by 1612. [Arbroath Burgh testimonial, 28 June 1612]

COLLIN, ALEXANDER, a militiaman burgess of Arbroath, 1685. [ACB]

COLVILLE, CHARLES, from Arbroath, a seaman aboard the Dolphin of Philadelphia, Captain O'Bryen, was captured and imprisoned in Algiers in 1785, later ransomed and returned to Scotland in 1790. [AJ.2230]

COLVILL, JOHN, deacon of the hammer-men of Arbroath, 1681. [HHA.157]

COLVILLE, JOHN, town clerk of Arbroath, 1788; born 1764, died 1812, husband of Catherine Mudie. [Arbroath Abbey MI][NAS.CS271.34688]

COLVILLE, ROBERT, landowner of Burnton, 1770. [DLS. 26]

COLVILL, THOMAS, hearth tax, St Vigeans, 1691. [NAS.E69.11.1]

COLVILL, THOMAS, of Brunton, a burgess of Arbroath, 1698. [ACB]

COLVILL, WILLIAM, a burgess of Arbroath, 1689; hearth tax, 1691. [ACB][NAS.E69.11.1]

CONSTABLE, GILBERT, master of the 75 ton Clementina of Arbroath, trading with France, 1725. [NAS.CE70.1.1]

COOK, ALEXANDER, in Muirden, Arbroath, 1752. [AER]

COOK, JAMES, a merchant in Arbroath, testament, 1739, Comm. St Andrews. [NAS]

COOK, THOMAS, in Seagait, Arbroath, 1658. [RGS.X.640]

COOPER, JAMES, a merchant in Arbroath, sasine, 1773. [NAS.RS35.24.221/413]

COORIE, JOHN, an officer of the shoe-makers craft in Arbroath, 1753. [AER.94]

COPLAND, JOHN, in Aberdeen, a burgess of Arbroath, 1792. [AA.18.941]

CORSAR, JOHN, a weaver burgess of Arbroath, 1797. [AA.18.941]

COSANS, JOHN, a brewer burgess of Arbroath, 1797. [AA.18.941]

COULL, ISABEL, hearth tax, Arbirlot, 1691. [NAS.E69.11.1]
COUPAR, JAMES, hearth tax, St Vigeans, 1691. [NAS.E69.11.1]
COUPER, JOHN, a weaver in Arbroath, 1745. [AER.93]
COUTTS, JAMES, a mason in Arbroath, a Jacobite in 1745. [JA]
COWLET, SAMUEL NORMAN, a burgess of Arbroath, 1798. [AA.18.941]
COWLEY, JOHN, a merchant in London, a burgess of Arbroath, 1791. [AA.18.941]
COWPAR, JOHN, a blacksmith in Arbroath, a Jacobite in 1745. [JA]
CRABB, ROBERT, a land-waiter in Montrose, a burgess of Arbroath, 1789. [AA.18.941]
CRAICK, DAVID, a weaver burgess of Arbroath, 1799. [AA.18.941]
CRAICK, PETER, a weaver burgess of Arbroath, 1799. [AA.18.941]
CRAIG, PETER, a weaver burgess of Arbroath, 1799. [AA.18.941]
CRAIGH, JOHN, servant to the Earl of Panmure, a burgess of Arbroath, 1698. [ACB]
CRAIK,........, a burgess of Arbroath, 1606. [HHA.143]
CRAMOND, JAMES, hearth tax, Arbirlot, 1691. [NAS.E69.11.1]
CRAMOND, JAMES, hearth tax, St Vigeans, 1691. [NAS.E69.11.1]
CRAMOND, JAMES, a glover in Arbroath, 1730s. [AER.95]
CRAMOND, JOHN, hearth tax, Arbroath, 1691. [NAS.E69.11.1]
CRAWFORD, HENRY, of Monorgan, hearth tax, St Vigeans, 1691. [NAS.E69.11.1]
CRAWFORD, ROBERT, in Hopehead of Arbroath, testament, 1734, Comm. St Andrews. [NAS]
CRAWFORD, ..., of Seaton, Justice of the Peace in Arbroath, 1686. [RPCS.XI.574]
CREE, JAMES, a mariner in Arbroath, and his spouse Jean Mitchell, testament, 1791, Comm. St Andrews. [NAS]
CRICHTON, ABRAHAM, a bailie burgess of Arbroath, 1599; testament, 1606, Comm. St Andrews. [NAS] [RGS.VI.1155]
CRICHTON, ALEXANDER, a mason in Arbroath, sasine, 1750. [NAS.RS35.17.224, etc]

CRICHTON, ALEXANDER, a shoe-maker burgess and freeman of Arbroath, 1789. [Arbroath Abbey MI]

CRIGHTON, DAVID, hearth tax, Arbirlot, 1691. [NAS.E69.11.1]

CRIGHTON, DAVID, a weaver in Arbroath, 1768. [AER.93]

CRICHTON, JAMES, a shoe-maker in Arbroath, a Jacobite in 1745, transported to Maryland. [JA][TNA.T1.328]

CRIGHTON, NICOLL, hearth tax, Arbirlot, 1691. [NAS.E69.11.1]

CRICHTON, THOMAS, a mason in Arbroath, sasine,1745, a Jacobite in 1745. [JA][NAS.RS35.19.302]

CRICHTON, WILLIAM, a shoe-maker in Arbroath, 1746. [AER.94]

CRICHTON, WILLIAM, born 1766, shipmaster in Arbroath, died 1800, husband of Mary Hackney, born 1761, died 1837. [Arbroath Abbey MI]

CRISTALL, JAMES, hearth tax, St Vigeans, 1691. [NAS.E69.11.1][NAS.E326.1.133]

CROOKSHANKS, CHARLES, a weaver burgess of Arbroath, 1797. [AA.18.941]

CRUICKSHANK, DAVID, a burgess of Arbroath, 1601. [RGS.VI.1155]

CRUICKSHANK, GEORGE, school-master of Arbroath, minister at Arbroath from 1738 until 1748. [F.5.424]

CRUIKSHANK, WALTER, a burgess of Arbroath, 1690. [ACB]

CUKEMAN, NICOLAS, in 'Fundie-Cuits', Arbroath, 1658. [RGS.X.640]

CUMMINGS, JOHN, a weaver burgess of Arbroath, 1797. [AA.18.941]

CUPAR, ROBERT, hearth tax, St Vigeans, 1691. [NAS.E69.11.1]

CURRIE, JOHN, a barber burgess of Arbroath, 1797. [AA.18.941]

CUTHBERT, JAMES, hearth tax, St Vigeans, 1691. [NAS.E69.11.1]

DAKERS, JAMES, a burgess of Arbroath, 1692. [ACB]

DAKERS, JAMES, a brewer in Arbroath, 1758, husband of Katherine Gowans, a sasine,1766. [NAS.E326.1.133; RS35.21.451]

DALGITY, ALEXANDER, a baker burgess of Arbroath, 1796. [AA.18.941]

DALGETTY, HERCULES, a burgess of Arbroath, husband of Barbara Haills, a sasine, 1620. [NAS.RS35.S1.141]
DALGETTY, JAMES, town clerk and notary public, 1674/1681, hearth tax, Arbroath, 1691. [NAS.E69.11.1] [HHA.157]
DALGETTY, JAMES, a baker in Arbroath, a letter, 1723. [NAS.B59.38.2.105]
DALGETTY, JOHN, a councillor of Arbroath, 1657. [HHA. 157]
DALGETTY, JOHN, a tide-waiter in Arbroath, 1765-1766. [NAS.CE70.1.4]
DALGETY, JOHN, a vintner in Arbroath, testament, 1774, Comm. St Andrews. [NAS]
DALGITY, JOHN, a watch-maker burgess of Arbroath, 1797. [AA.18.941]
DALGETTY, MARGARET, hearth tax, Arbroath, 1691. [NAS.E69.11.1]
DALGITY, THOMAS, a shoe-maker burgess of Arbroath, 1797. [AA.18.941]
DALL, ALEXANDER, hearth tax, Arbirlot, 1691. [NAS.E69.11.1]
DALL, ANDREW, hearth tax, Arbroath, 1691. [NAS.E69.11.1]
DALL, JOHN, in Milneden, a burgess of Arbroath, 1683. [ACB]
DALL, ROBERT, a merchant in Arbroath, husband of Elizabeth Guthrie, parents of John, Charles, Mary, Elizabeth, and Margaret, 1729, 1730. [NAS.AC9.1083, 1109; GD3.14.2.1.45]
DALL, WILLIAM, an officer of the shoemakers craft in Arbroath, 1761. [AER.94]
DANCERS, JOHN, a heckler burgess of Arbroath, 1797. [AA. 18.941]
DARGIE, ANDREW, born 1701, a slater in Arbroath, died 1780, husband of Katherine Hay, born 1706, died 1768. [Arbroath Abbey MI]
DARGIE, JAMES, born 1735, master of the John and Katherine of Arbroath, trading with Danzig 1767; died off Borholm, Sweden, 1785, husband of Agnes Renny. [NAS.CE53.1.6][Arbroath Abbey MI]
DAVIDSON, HENRY, a burgess of Arbroath, 1687; hearth tax, 1691. [ACB][NAS.E69.11.1]

DAVIDSON, HENRY, a weaver in Arbroath, sasine,1718.
[NAS.RS35.13.227]
DAVIDSON, JAMES, a burgess of Arbroath, 1687. [ACB]
DAVIDSON, JOHN, hearth tax, Arbirlot, 1691.
[NAS.E69.11.1]
DAVIDSON, PATRICK, hearth tax, Arbirlot, 1691.
[NAS.E69.11.1]
DAVIDSON, ROBERT, hearth tax, Arbirlot, 1691.
[NAS.E69.11.1]
DAVIDSON, ROBERT, a shoe-maker in Arbroath, 1769.
[AER.94]
DAVIDSON, WILLIAM, Captain of Lord Lindsay's Regiment of Foot, a burgess of Arbroath 1797. [ACB]
DEANS, ALEXANDER, hearth tax, Arbroath, 1691.
[NAS.E69.11.1]
DEANS, JAMES, a burgess of Arbroath, 1686. [ACB]
DEALL, ANDREW, hearth tax, Arbirlot, 1691.
[NAS.E69.11.1]
DEAR, DAVID, a weaver burgess of Arbroath, 1796. [AA. 18.941]
DE'ERVAL, Count ROBERT, a burgess of Arbroath, 1790.
[AA.18.941]
DEUCHAR, DAVID, a burgess of Arbroath, 1688. [ACB]
DEUCHAR, DAVID, a seal-engraver burgess of Arbroath, 1789. [AA.18.941]
DEUCHAR, JAMES, a land-labourer in Arbroath, 1724.
[NAS.GD3.14.2.1.44]
DEUCHARS, WILLIAM, hearth tax, Arbirlot, 1691.
[NAS.E69.11.1]
DICK, ANDREW, a mariner in Arbroath, husband of Margaret Spink, parents of Hannah and Mary, deed 1770.
[NAS.CS237.D.5.20]
DICKIESON, WILLIAM, hearth tax, Arbroath, 1691.
[NAS.E69.11.1]
DINGWALL, ALEXANDER, a land labourer in Arbroath, relict Margaret Miller, testament, 1775,
Comm. St Andrews. [NAS]
DODIE, JAMES, hearth tax, Arbroath, 1691. [NAS.E69.11.1]
DOER, ANDREW, hearth tax, St Vigeans, 1691.
[NAS.E69.11.1]
DOER, WILLIAM, hearth tax, St Vigeans, 1691.
[NAS.E69.11.1]
DOIG, ALEXANDER, a glover in Arbroath, 1738. [AER.95]

DOIG, DAVID, in Arbroath, 1724. [NAS.GD3.14.2.1.44]
DOIG, JAMES, hearth tax, Arbroath, 1691. [NAS.E69.11.1]
DOIG, JAMES, a merchant in Arbroath, 1744.
[NAS.AC11.162]
DOIG, JOHN, of Suirds, a burgess of Arbroath, 1696. [ACB]
DOIG, Reverend ROBERT, a burgess of Arbroath, 1791.
[AA.18.941]
DOIG, WILLIAM, a burgess of Arbroath, 1789. [AA.18.941]
DORMAN, DAVID, a burgess of Arbroath, a Jacobite in 1745.
[JA]
DORRATT, DAVID, landowner, 1770. [DLS.26]
DORRITT, HENRY, a skipper of Arbroath, master of the
Mary of Arbroath, 1731, and later master of the
Catharine of Arbroath, 1737. [NAS.CE53.1.2; AC8/549]
DORRETT, JOHN, hearth tax, Arbroath, 1691.
[NAS.E69.11.1]
DORRETT, PATRICK, hearth tax, Arbirlot, 1691.
[NAS.E69.11.1]
DORWARD, ALEXANDER, a burgess of Arbroath, 1692.
[ACB]
DORWARD, ALEXANDER, a shoe-maker in Arbroath, 1739,
boxmaster of the craft, 1754. [AER.94]
DORWARD, DAVID, a land labourer in Arbroath, a Jacobite
in 1745. [JA]
DORWARD, DAVID, a weaver in Arbroath, a Jacobite in
1745. [JA]
DORWARD, GEORGE, in New Grange, Arbroath, testament,
1606, Comm. St Andrews. [NAS]
DORWARD, GEORGE, a weaver in Arbroath 1742, box-
master of the craft, 1768. [AER.93]
DORWARD, JAMES, a burgess of Arbroath, 1642. [NAS.
Retours, Perth]
DORWARD, JAMES, a carter in Arbroath, sasine, 1779.
[NAS.RS35.27.392]
DORWARD, JOHN, a burgess of Arbroath, 1688. [ACB]
DORWARD, JOHN, a merchant burgess of Arbroath, 1690.
[ACB]
DORWARD, JOHN, hearth tax, St Vigeans, 1691.
[NAS.E69.11.1]
DORWARD, JOHN, servant to James Peirson of Balmadies, a
burgess of Arbroath, 1697. [ACB]
DORWARD, JOHN, born 1714, died 1785, husband of
Christian Smith, born 1731, died 1786, parents of John,

James, Alexander, Charles, Robert, Helen, Isobel, Jean, William, Alison, and Margaret. [Arbirlot MI]

DOWIE, ALEXANDER, a weaver in Arbroath, 1768. [AER. 93]

DOWIE, HENRY, hearth tax, St Vigeans, 1691. [NAS.E69.11.1]

DRUMMOND, JOHN, a merchant from Edinburgh, a burgess of Arbroath, 1685. [ACB]

DRYBURGH, DAVID, a weaver burgess of Arbroath, testament, 1662, Comm. St Andrews. [NAS]

DUMBRANK, WILLIAM, a weaver burgess of Arbroath, 1798. [AA.18.941]

DUN, WILLIAM, a merchant in Forfar, a burgess of Arbroath, 1789. [AA.18.941]

DUNCAN, ALEXANDER, hearth tax, Arbirlot, 1691. [NAS.E69.11.1]

DUNCAN, ALEXANDER, a burgess of Arbroath, 1692. [ACB]

DUNCAN, ALEXANDER, a weaver in Arbroath, 1737. [AER.93]

DUNCAN, ALEXANDER, a skipper in Arbroath, testament, 1803, Comm. St Andrews. [NAS]

DUNCAN, ANDREW, hearth tax, St Vigeans, 1691. [NAS.E69.11.1]

DUNCAN, ANDREW, a skipper burgess of Arbroath, 1796. [AA.18.941]

DUNCAN, DAVID, a weaver in Arbroath, 1745. [AER.93]

DUNCAN, JAMES, a burgess of Arbroath, husband of Elspeth Dall, a sasine, 1690. [NAS.RS35.S3.VIII.132]

DUNCAN, JAMES, hearth tax, Arbirlot, 1691. [NAS.E69.11.1]

DUNCAN, JAMES, tenant of land in Punderlawfield and Keptie, Arbroath, 1716. [NAS.E650/2]

DUNCAN, JAMES, from Arbroath, a sailor in London, 1750. [NAS.S/H]

DUNCAN, JAMES, a wright burgess of Arbroath, 1797. [AA.18.941]

DUNCAN, JOHN, a councillor of Arbroath, and deacon of the glovers there, 1680. [HHA.157/189]

DUNCAN, JOHN, from Dundee, a burgess of Arbroath, 1690. [ACB]

DUNCAN, JOHN, hearth tax, Arbroath, 1691.
[NAS.E69.11.1]
DUNCAN, JOHN, a brewer in Arbroath, a Jacobite in 1745.
[JA]
DUNCAN, MARGARET, hearth tax, Arbroath, 1691.
[NAS.E69.11.1]
DUNCAN, PATRICK, hearth tax, St Vigeans, 1691.
[NAS.E69.11.1]
DUNCAN, PATRICK, in Newton, a burgess of Arbroath, 1698. [ACB]
DUNCAN, PETER, ground labourer in Arbroath, husband of Elisabeth Brown, born 1750, died 1787. [Arbroath Abbey MI]
DUNCAN, ROBERT, a tailor burgess of Arbroath, 1797. [AA. 18.941]
DUNCAN, THOMAS, by the Brothock Water, 1658. [RGS.X.640]
DUNGAR, DAVID, hearth tax, Arbroath, 1691.
[NAS.E69.11.1]
DUNLOP, THOMAS, a burgess of Arbroath, a sasine, 1620.
[NAS.RS35.S1.1.164]
DUNLOP, THOMAS, a councillor of Arbroath, 1657.
[RGS.X.640]
DUNLOP, THOMAS, in Arbroath, sasine, 1733.
[NAS.RS35.15.37]
DURIE, JAMES, a burgess of Arbroath, testament, 1600, Comm. St Andrews. [NAS]
DURIE, SIMON, son of John Durie minister at Montrose, graduated MA from St Andrews University in 1600, minister at Arbroath from 1628 to 1653, a burgess of Arbroath, 1630, husband of Christian Maule. [HHA.183] [F.5.424]
EASSIE, JAMES, a burgess of Arbroath, 1682. [ACB]
EASSIE, JOHN, son of William Eassie a weaver burgess of Arbroath, heir to his grandfather John Aikman a burgess of Arbroath, 1665. [NAS,Forfar.Retours]
EASSIE, WILLIAM, a weaver burgess of Arbroath, husband of Nicola Aikman, parents of John Eassie, 1665; sasine, 1667. [NAS. Forfar. Retours; RS35.S3.III.134]
EDGAR, Bishop HARRY, born 1695 son of David Edgar of Keithock, an Episcopal minister in Arbroath, died 1765, his wife Barbara Rait, daughter of Reverend William Rait in Monikie, born 1693, died 1774, testament, 1769, Comm. St Andrews. [NAS]

EDGAR, PATRICK, servant to Patrick Anton, a burgess of Arbroath, 1698. [ACB]

EDISON, ALEXANDER, a burgess of Arbroath, 1692. [ACB]

EDISON, DAVID, hearth tax, St Vigeans, 1691; a weaver in Barngreen, a burgess of Arbroath, husband of Jean Shippard, sasine, 1695. [NAS.RS35.S3.IX.545; E69.11.1]

EDWARDS, FRANCIS, of the General Post Office in Edinburgh, a burgess of Arbroath, 1790. [AA.18.941]

EDWARDS, JEREMIAH, of the frigate Champion, a burgess of Arbroath, 1790. [AA.18.941]

ELLIOT, ANDREW, a burgess of Arbroath, husband of Janet Livingstone, testament, 1599, Comm. St Andrews. [NAS]

ELLIOT, ANDREW, burgess of Arbroath, 1601, councillor there in 1617, baillie in 1624. [HHA.138/150] [RGS.VIII.841]

ELLIOT, ANDREW, of Cuithly, a burgess of Arbroath, 1649. [RGS.IX.2136]

ELLIOT, ANDREW, burgess of Arbroath, testament, Comm. St Andrews, [NAS]; relict Agnes Wood, sasine, 1650. [NAS.RS35.S2.III.227]

ENGLISH, JAMES, master of the Two Sisters of Arbroath, trading with Norway, and of the Jean of Arbroath, trading with the Netherlands in 1749, 1753. [NAS.E504.24.2; E326.1.133]

ENGLISH, JOHN, master of the John of Arbroath, 1725. [NAS.E508]

ENGLISH, WILLIAM, master of the Two Sisters of Arbroath, 1749. [NAS.E504.24.2]

ENSLIE, JOHN, a merchant in Rotterdam, the Netherlands, a burgess of Arbroath, 1791. [AA.18.941]

ERSKINE, CHARLES, Earl of Mar, a burgess of Arbroath, 1678. [NAS.GD2.10.271]

ERSKINE, Lord JOHN, a burgess of Arbroath, 1678. [NAS.GD23.10.271]

ERSKINE, WILLIAM, a merchant in Arbroath, 1677. [NAS.AC7.4]

ERSKINE, ..., of Kirkbuddo, Justice of the Peace in Arbroath, 1686. [RPCS.XI.574]

ERVETT, DAVID, a burgess of Arbroath, 1687. [ACB]

ESPLIN, AGNES, hearth tax, Arbroath, 1691. [NAS.E69.11.1]

ESPLIN, ALEXANDER, a burgess of Arbroath, 1697. [ACB]

ESPLIN, ALEXANDER, a manufacturer burgess of Arbroath, 1796. [AA.18.941]
ESPLIN, ANDREW, hearth tax, St Vigeans, 1691. [NAS.E69.11.1]
ESPLIN, DAVID, a tailor in Arbroath, 1688. [AA.A1.1455]
ESPLIN, JAMES, a burgess of Arbroath, spouse Margaret Johnston, testament, 1657, Comm. Brechin. [NAS]
ESPLIN, JAMES, a burgess of Arbroath, son of James Esplin a burgess of Arbroath, dead by 1663; sasine, 1666. [NAS.Forfar. Retours; RS35.S3.III.223]
ESPLIN, JAMES, a tailor burgess of Arbroath, 1685, hearth tax, Arbroath, 1691; testament, 1691, Comm. St Andrews. [NAS.69.11.1]
ESPLIN, JAMES, a burgess of Arbroath, 1698, sasines, 1702, 1704. [NAS.RS35.10.363]
ESPLIN, JOHN, a burgess of Arbroath, 1692. [ACB]
ESPLIN, WILLIAM, master of the Elizabeth of Arbroath trading to the Netherlands and Norway, 1680s. [NAS.E72.7.5/7; E72.16.6/7/11]
ESPLIN, WILLIAM, a merchant burgess of Arbroath, testament, 1686, Comm. St Andrews. [NAS]
ESSIE, JAMES, sr., a weaver in Arbroath, a Jacobite in 1745; 1748. [JA][AER.93]
ESSIE, JOHN, born 1656, a weaver burgess of Arbroath, died 1728, husband of Janet Chepland born 1649, died 1724. [Arbroath Abbey MI]
ESSIE, JOHN, sr., a weaver in Arbroath, 1748. [AER.93]
ESSON, COLIN, a burgess of Arbroath, 1694. [ACB]
ESTON, DAVID, a weaver burgess of Arbroath, 1797. [AA. 18.941]
ESTON, JOHN, a burgess of Arbroath, 1793. [AA.18.941]
FAIRFOULL, WILLIAM, son of William Fairfoull, a surgeon apothecary of Arbroath, 1708. [NAS.AC8/98]
FAIRWEATHER, JAMES, a burgess of Arbroath, 1692. [ACB]
FAIRWEATHER, THOMAS, a merchant from Montrose, a burgess of Arbroath, 1686. [ACB]
FAIRWEATHER, Mr THOMAS, of Idvie, a Notary Public, a burgess of Arbroath, 1681; a Justice of the Peace in Arbroath, 1686. [RPCS.XI.574][HHA.157][ACB]
FAIRWEATHER, Mr THOMAS, tenant of land in Tarrie, Arbroath, 1716. [NAS.E650/2]

FALCONER, GEORGE, a currier in Arbroath, sasine,1780. [NAS.RS35.28.191]

FARQUHAR, JOHN, servant of Robert Forbes of Learnie, a burgess of Arbroath, 1699. [ACB]

FARQUHAR, MARGARET, hearth tax, Arbroath, 1691. [NAS.E69.11.1]

FARQUHAR, WILLIAM, a burgess of Arbroath, 1687. [ACB]

FARQUHARSON, WILLIAM, a merchant in Arbroath, son of David Farquharson of Kinneries, sasine, 1718. [NAS.RS35.13.191, etc]

FAULD, JAMES, a merchant in Arbroath, 1737, 1738, 1749. [NAS.AC8.549, 565; AC9.1661]

FAULD, PATRICK, hearth tax, Arbirlot, 1691. [NAS.E69.11.1]

FERGUSON, DAVID, a weaver in Arbroath, 1742. [AER.93]

FERGUSON, JAMES, deacon of the tailors in Arbroath, 1681. [HHA.157]

FERGUSON, JOHN, born 1655, a minister at Arbroath from 1699 until 1737, husband of [1] Margaret McDougall, Bethia Brand; testament, 1745, Comm. St Andrews. [NAS][F.5.424]

FERGUSON, WILLIAM, an Excise officer in Arbroath, a Jacobite in 1745. [JA]

FERGUSON, ..., landowner of Lochlands, 1770. [DLS.26]

FERRIER, CHARLES, box-master of the shoemakers in Arbroath, 1753-1755. [AER.94]

FERRIER, CHARLES, a weaver burgess of Arbroath, 1797. [AA.18.941]

FERRIER, ISOBEL, hearth tax, Arbroath, 1691. [NAS.E69.11.1]

FERRIER, JAMES, a burgess of Arbroath, 1683. [ACB]

FERRIER, JAMES, a mariner from Arbroath, died aboard HMS Vanguard, probate, 1694, PCC. [TNA]

FERRIER, JAMES, a shoe-maker in Arbroath, 1737. [AER.94]

FERRIER, JOHN, hearth tax, St Vigeans, 1691. [NAS.E69.11.1]

FERRIER, ROBERT, a farmer in Arbroath, a Jacobite in 1745. [JA]

FERRIER, ROBERT, an officer of the shoe-makers craft of Arbroath, 1754. [AER.94]

FERRIER, SAMUEL, a weaver burgess of Arbroath, 1799. [AA.18.941]
FETHIE, CHARLES, a burgess of Arbroath, testament, 1616, Comm. St Andrews. [NAS]
FETHIE, JAMES, a cordiner burgess of Arbroath, 1606. [ACB]
FIFE, DAVID, a merchant burgess of Arbroath, 1791. [AA.18.941]
FINDLAY, ALEXANDER, deacon of the tailors of Arbroath, 1680. [HHA.289]
FINLAY, DAVID, hearth tax, St Vigeans, 1691. [NAS.E69.11.1]
FINDLAY, GEORGE, master of the Margaret of Auchmithie, 1747. [NAS.E504.24.1]
FINDLAY, JOHN, hearth tax, St Vigeans, 1691. [NAS.E69.11.1]
FINDLAY, PATRICK, a merchant burgess of Arbroath, 1797. [AA.18.941]
FINDLAY, ROBERT, a weaver burgess of Arbroath, 1797. [AA.18.941]
FINDLOW, JOHN, a thatcher in Arbroath, spouse of Isobel Allan, daughter of John Allan a burgess of Arbroath, a sasine 1672. [NAS.RS35.S3.V.172]
FITCHET, ALEXANDER, a burgess of Arbroath, 1696. [ACB]
FITCHET, ALEXANDER, a glover in Arbroath, 1745. [AER.95]
FITCHET, JOHN, a tailor from Grangepans, a burgess of Arbroath, 1791. [AA.18.941]
FITCHET, WILLIAM, a merchant and bailie of Arbroath, born 1716, died1796; testament, 1800, Comm. St Andrews. [NAS.E326.1.133] [Arbroath Abbey MI]
FITHIE, HENRY, of Peebles, by Arbroath, Parliamentary Commissioner for Arbroath 1667-1669, Provost 1677, Justice of the Peace in 1686, hearth tax, Arbroath, 1691. [NAS.E69.11.1; AC7.4][RPCS.XI.574][HHA.156/7]
FLEMING, JOHN, born 1702, master of a 9 ton boat of Arbroath, 1725, died 1779, husband of Catherine Bean. [NAS.AC9.945][Arbroath Abbey MI]
FLEMING, THOMAS, master of a 10 ton of Arbroath, 1725; master of the Jean of Arbroath, trading with Norway, and the Netherlands in 1740s, trading with the Netherlands in

1750, dead by 1753, husband of Ann Lawson.
[NAS.AC9.945; E504.24.1/2; CE53.1.4]
FLEMING, THOMAS, master of the Arbroath Packet, trading with Russia, 1771. [NAS.CE53.1.8]
FOORD, JAMES, hearth tax, St Vigeans, 1691.
[NAS.E69.11.1]
FORBES, JAMES, a merchant burgess of Arbroath, 1791.
[AA.18.941]
FORBES, JOHN, a merchant from Aberdeen, a burgess of Arbroath, 1687. [ACB]
FORBES, Mr ROBERT, of Learnie, a burgess of Arbroath, 1699. [ACB]
FORDELL, JOHN, hearth tax, Arbroath, 1691.
[NAS.E69.11.1]
FORDUE, JAMES, a wright in Arbroath, a Jacobite in 1745. [JA]
FORDYCE, JOHN, a burgess of Arbroath, 1688. [ACB]
FORDYCE, ..., in London, a burgess of Arbroath, 1791.
[AA.18.941]
FORREST, JOHN, a skipper in Arbroath, 1752. [AER.68]
FORRESTER, ALEXANDER, admitted as a burgess of Arbroath in 1764. [NAS.GD45.15.66]
FORRESTER, DAVID, a burgess of Arbroath, 1681. [ACB]
FORRET, ROBERT, a workman in Arbroath, testament, 1743, Comm. St Andrews. [NAS]
FOTHERINGHAM, DAVID, a merchant in Arbroath, spouse Elizabeth Ogilvie, sasines,1730, 1737, 1733-1740.
[NAS.RS35.14.575; AC9.1103; AC11/96; CE70.1.2]
FOTHERINGHAM, EUGENE, late master of the McKenzie of Arbroath, a galley, 1738. [NAS.AC9.1103]
FOULERTON, ANDREW, hearth tax, St Vigeans, 1691.
[NAS.E69.11.1]
FOWLER, ..., in Gallowden, Arbroath, 1752. [AER]
FRASER, DAVID, a skipper in Arbroath, master of the Concord of Arbroath, trading with Virginia, Riga, and New England, 1741, 1744. [NAS.CE53.1.3; AC11.160]
FRASER, JAMES, of Kirkton, educated at Marischal College in Aberdeen, minister at Arbroath from 1653 to 1668, died 1689, husband of Isobel Philip, parents of James. [F. 5.424]
FRASER, JOHN, of Kirkton, hearth tax, St Vigeans, 1691.
[NAS.E69.11.1][RPCS.XI.574]

FRASER, JOHN, of Hospitalfield, tenant of lands in Dishland, Arbroath, 1716. [NAS.E650/2]
FRASER, JOHN, master of the Concord of Arbroath, trading with New England and Maryland in 1744. [NAS.AC11/160; E504.24.1]
FRASER, JON., in Hercules Den, Arbroath, 1752. [AER]
FRASER, JOHN, a burgess of Arbroath, 1794. [AA.18.941]
FRASER, ..., landowner of Kirkton, 1770. [DLS.26]
FROST, JOHN, hearth tax, Arbroath, 1691. [NAS.E69.11.1]
FROST, JOHN, a burgess of Arbroath, husband of Elspeth Stell, sasine, 1698. [NAS.RS35.S3.X.51]
FULLERTON, DAVID, a burgess of Arbroath, 1689. [ACB]
FUTHIE, CHARLES, a burgess of Arbroath, his widow Alison Bruce testament, 1617, Comm. St Andrews. [NAS]
FUTHIE, DAVID, a burgess of Arbroath, testament, 1624, Comm. St Andrews. [NAS]
FYELL, WILLIAM, hearth tax, Arbirlot, 1691. [NAS.E69.11.1]
FYFFE, JAMES, hearth tax, Arbroath, 1691. [NAS.E69.11.1]
FYFFE, JOHN, hearth tax, Arbroath, 1691; a burgess of Arbroath, 1692. [ACB][NAS.E69.11.1]
FYFFE, PETER, hearth tax, Arbroath, 1691. [NAS.E69.11.1]
GAEN, JAMES, hearth tax, Arbroath, 1691. [NAS.E69.11.1]
GAIN, JOHN, a burgess of Arbroath, 1609. [RPCS.8.790]
GAIRDEN, JOHN, hearth tax, Arbroath, 1691. [NAS.E69.11.1]
GAIRDENER, JOHN, hearth tax, St Vigeans, 1691. [NAS.69.11.1]
GAIRDENER, WILLIAM, hearth tax, St Vigeans, 1691. [NAS.E69.11.1]
GAIRDNER, Provost JOHN, in Arbroath, 1753. [NAS.E326.1.133]
GAIRDYNE, JAMES, a burgess of Arbroath, 1693. [ACB]
GAIRN, JAMES, hearth tax, Arbroath, 1691. [NAS.E69.11.1]
GALL, JOHN, servant of the Earl of Northesk, a burgess of Arbroath, 1693. [ACB]
GARDEN, DAVID, master of a 10 ton boat of Arbroath, 1725, dead by 1752. [NAS.AC9.945][AER.79]
GARDINE, GILBERT, a burgess of Arbroath, 1606. [HHA.143][ACB]
GARDINE, JOHN, a burgess of Arbroath, testament, 1617. Comm. St Andrews. [NAS]

GARDINER, DAVID, hearth tax, St Vigeans, 1691.
[NAS.E69.11.1]
GARDINER, JOHN, landowner, 1770. [DLS.26]
GARDINER, ..., landowner of North Tarry, 1770. [DLS.26]
GARDNER, DAVID, master of the David of Arbroath, 1711.
[NAS.AC9/392]
GARDNER, GILBERT, a burgess of Arbroath, sasine, 1621.
[NAS.RS35.S1.1.185]
GARDNER, JOHN, a merchant in Arbroath, sasine,1742.
[NAS.RS35.16.134, etc]
GARDNER, JOHN, a weaver in South Tarry, died 1737. [St
Vigeans MI]
GARDNER, WILLIAM, a skipper in Arbroath, sasines,1771,
1776. [NAS.RS35.23.398, etc; S/H]
GARDNER, ..., master of the Margaret of Arbroath, in
Aberdeen, 1752. [AJ.222]
GARDYNE, JAMES, a merchant in Arbroath, sasines,1743,
1744. [NAS.AC9.1500; AC11.162; RS35.XVI.134/226]
GARDYNE, JAMES, of Middleton, parish of Arbroath,
testament, 1790, Comm. St Andrews. [NAS]
GARDYNE, ROBERT, son of James Gardyne, a baker in
Arbroath, 1699. [AA.A1.114.58]
GARDYNE, THOMAS, a burgess of Arbroath, 1674. [HHA]
GARDYNE, WILLIAM, a burgess of Arbroath, 1688. [ACB]
GARN, JOHN, hearth tax, St Vigeans, 1691. [NAS.E69.11.1]
GARRIE, HENRY, a burgess of Arbroath, 1688. [ACB]
GARRIOCH, WILLIAM, a skipper in Arbroath, 1722; master
of the Elizabeth of Arbroath, 1751. [NAS.AC9.839;
E504.1.4]
GAULL, JAMES, master of the Marshall of Arbroath, 1743.
[NAS.E54.24.1].
GAWN, JAMES, hearth tax, Arbroath, 1691. [NAS.E69.11.1]
GEEKIE, JAMES, a surgeon in Arbroath, dead by 1744,
husband of Katherine Wallace, parents of William and
Mary, 1744. [NAS.AC11.160]
GEEKIE, WILLIAM, from Arbroath, sailor in the Royal
Navy before 1763, settled in Goose Creek, South
Carolina, as a planter, a Loyalist in 1776, returned to
Arbroath by 1784; a merchant in Arbroath, testament,
1793, Comm. St Andrews. [TNA.AO.12.50.138, etc]
[NAS.CS97.103.7]
GELLATLY, JOHN, a burgess of Arbroath, 1687; hearth tax,
Arbroath, 1691. [ACB][NAS.E69.11.1]

GELLATLY, JOHN, a bailie in Arbroath, testament, 1735, Comm. St Andrews. [NAS]
GELLATLY, JOHN, a merchant in Arbroath, 1744, provost sasine,1753. [NAS.AC11.162; RS35.XIV.566; E326.1.133]
GELLATLY, THOMAS, a merchant bailie of Arbroath, co-owner of the St Thomas of Arbroath, husband of Isobel Lyell, sasine,1743, 1744, 1753, 1756. [NAS.AC11.162; E326.1.133; RS35.XVIII.345; GD45.23.110]
GELLATLY, ..., master of the Arbroath, lost at sea when returning from Virginia, 1752. [AJ.222]
GEORGE, JOHN, a burgess of Arbroath, 1686. [ACB]
GIB, WILLIAM, Customs Surveyor at Montrose, burgess of Arbroath, 1796. [AA.18.941]
GIBSON, ALEXANDER, a burgess of Arbroath, 1696. [ACB]
GIBSON, DAVID, a smith, hearth tax, Arbroath, 1691; deacon of the hammermen of Arbroath, 1702, father of John born 1685, died 1702. [NAS.E69.11.1][Arbroath Abbey MI]
GIBSON, GEORGE, a burgess of Arbroath, 1692. [ACB]
GIBSON, HARRY, a skipper from St Andrews, a burgess of Arbroath, 1684, master of the Catherine of Arbroath, 1684, and of the Agnes of Arbroath, trading with the Netherlands and Norway. [ACB][NAS.RD2.67.46; RD4.57.641; E72.7.15; E72.13.14/15/16]
GIBSON, JAMES, in Arbroath, 1664. [NAS.GD45.16.1225]
GIBSON, JAMES, a burgess of Arbroath, 1692. [ACB]
GIBSON, JOHN, hearth tax, Arbroath, 1691. [NAS.E69.11.1]
GIBSON, JOHN, a weaver in Almerieclose, sasine, 1774. [NAS.RS35.XXV.439]
GIBSON, PATRICK, a weaver burgess of Arbroath, 1795. [AA.18.941]
GIBSON, WILLIAM, the younger, master of the Catherine of Arbroath trading with Norway in 1684, later master of the Agnes of Arbroath trading with the Netherlands and Norway 1685. [NAS.E72.7.15; E72.13.14/15/16]
GIBSON, WILLIAM, deacon of the weaver trade, husband of Isabel Neish, 1788. [Arbroath Abbey MI]
GILLESPIE, JOHN, master of the John of Arbroath, 1716; master of the Two Brothers of Arbroath trading with Holland, Norway, Ireland and Riga,1740s; master of the Catherine of Arbroath, 1749, husband of Margaret Lamb, parents of Agnes, James, John, Katherine, and Mary,

sasines; died on voyage from Rotterdam in 1746.
[NAS.AC9.567; CE53.1.3/4; E504.24.1/2; E504.1.1;
RS35.XXI.495, etc]

GILLESPIE, JOHN, a mariner in Arbroath, son of John
Gillespie a skipper there and his wife Margaret Lamb,
sasine,1766. [NAS.RS35.21.495]

GILLESPIE, WILLIAM, a burgess of Arbroath, 1682. [ACB]
hearth tax, Arbroath, 1691. [NAS.E69.11.1]

GILLESPIE, WILLIAM, master of the Mary of Arbroath,
1716. [NAS.AC9.567]

GILLESPIE, WILLIAM, born 1721, son of William Gillespie
and his wife Janet Mitchell, a sailor in Arbroath, a
Jacobite in 1745. [JA]

GILLIEVRAY, ARCHIBALD, a merchant burgess of
Arbroath, 1797. [AA.18.941]

GLEIG, Reverend GEORGE, a burgess of Arbroath, 1791.
[AA.18.941]; born 1757 in Brechin, son of George Gleig
a blacksmith, graduated MA in Aberdeen 1777, minister
at Arbroath, 1788 until 1835, husband of Mary Duncan,
parents of Jean, Helen, Mary, Margaret, Ann Forbes,
Jonathan Duncan, Alexdrina, George and Michie. [F.
5.425]

GOLD, ALEXANDER, a flax-dresser burgess of Arbroath,
1797. [AA.18.941]

GOODALE, JAMES, a merchant burgess of Arbroath, 1799.
[AA.18.941]

GOODALE, MARGARET, hearth tax, St Vigeans, 1691.
[NAS.E69.11.1]

GORDON, Sir ALEXANDER, of Auchentoule, Senator of the
Court of Justice, a burgess of Arbroath, 1688. [ACB]

GORDON, ALEXANDER, son of the above, a burgess of
Arbroath, 1688. [ACB]

GORDON, ANDREW, a burgess of Arbroath, 1797. [AA.
18.941]

GORDON, DAVID, Captain of the 134th Regiment, a burgess
of Arbroath, 1795. [AA.18.941]

GORDON, HUGH, servant of Sir Alexander Gordon, a
burgess of Arbroath, 1682. [ACB]

GORDON, JOHN, of Colliston, Justice of the Peace in
Arbroath, 1686, hearth tax, St Vigeans, 1691.
[NAS.E69.11.1][RPCS.XI.574]

GORDON, JOHN, a white ironsmith burgess of Arbroath,
1797. [AA.18.941]

GORDON, PATRICK, school-master in Monifieth, a burgess of Arbroath, 1789. [AA.18.941]

GOUCK, ALEXANDER, a burgess of Arbroath, 1696. [ACB]

GOUCK, FRANCIS, servant to Robert Forbes of Lernie, a burgess of Arbroath, 1699. [ACB]

GOUK, JOHN, hearth tax, St Vigeans, 1691. [NAS.E69.11.1]

GOULD, WALTER, a weaver in Stotfield, a burgess of Arbroath, 1699. [ACB]

GOURLAW, DAVID, in Inverkeilor, a burgess of Arbroath, 1687. [ACB]

GOURLAY, DAVID, born 1752, a skipper in Arbroath, died 1840, husband of Jean Clark. [Arbroath Abbey MI]

GOURLAY, DAVID, born 1752, a skipper in Arbroath, died 1840, spouse of Jean Clark. [Arbroath Abbey MI]

GOURLAY, JANET, born 1749, died 1804. [Arbroath Abbey MI]

GOURLAY, JOHN, hearth tax, St Vigeans, 1691. [NAS.E69.11.1]

GOW, GEORGE, a merchant burgess of Arbroath, 1790. [AA.18.941]

GOW, JAMES, a merchant burgess of Arbroath, 1797. [AA.18.941]

GOW, JOHN, a merchant burgess of Arbroath, 1797. [AA.18.941]

GOW, WILLIAM, a merchant burgess of Arbroath, 1795. [AA.18.941]

GOW, HARRIS, and Company, tanners in Arbroath, 1797. [NAS.CS230.SEQNS.G1.9]

GOWANS, ALEXANDER, a millwright burgess of Arbroath, 1797. [AA.18.941]

GOWANS, ANDREWS, hearth tax, St Vigeans, 1691. [NAS.E69.11.1]

GOWANS, JAMES, in Arbroath, 1664. [NAS.GD45.16.1225]

GOWANS, JAMES, hearth tax, St Vigeans, 1691. [NAS.E69.11.1]

GOWANS, JAMES, in Wardmilne of Arbroath, and spouse Margaret Ritchie, sasine, 1724. [NAS.RS35.13.586, etc]

GOWANS, JAMES, in Muirden, Arbroath, 1752. [AER]

GOWANS, JOHN, a burgess of Arbroath, 1684, hearth tax, Arbroath, 1691. [ACB][NAS.E69.11.1]

GOWAN, JOHN, hearth tax, St Vigeans, 1691. [NAS.E69.11.1]

GOWANS, JOHN, a shoemaker in Arbroath, 1759. [AER.94]

GOWANS, JOHN, a weaver in Arbroath, 1766. [AER.93]
GOWANS, Reverend JOHN, in Lunan, a burgess of Arbroath, 1791. [AA.18.941]
GOWANS, MARION, in Muirden, Arbroath, 1752. [AER]
GOWANS, THOMAS, a baxter burgess of Arbroath, 1795. [AA.18.941]
GOWRIE, DAVID, a shoe-maker burgess of Arbroath, 1797. [AA.18.941]
GRAHAME, ALEXANDER, a tenant of Pearson's acres in Arbroath, 1716. [NAS.E650/2]
GRAHAM, ALEXANDER, son of Alexander Graham of Duntrune, a merchant in Arbroath, sasine,1768. [NAS.RS35.22.482; E326.1.133; GD45.16.272]
GRAHAM, Captain, a merchant in Arbroath, and spouse Clementina Gardyne, sasine, 1768. [NAS.RS35.22.482]
GRAHAM, WILLIAM, of Morphie, landowner of Almerieclose, 1770. [DLS.26]
GRAINGER, DAVID, school-master of Arbroath, testament, 1682. Comm. St Andrews. [NAS]
GRAINGER, JOHN, a bailie of Arbroath, 1617. [HHA. 149/150]
GRANGE, DAVID, Alexander, and Cirsten, hearth tax, Arbroath, 1691. [NAS.E69.11.1]
GRANT, DAVID, a merchant burgess of Arbroath, 1794. [AA. 18.941]
GRANT, ELIZABETH, hearth tax, Arbroath, 1691. [NAS.E69.11.1]
GRANT, FERGUS, a weaver burgess of Arbroath, 1791. [AA. 18.941]
GRANT, GEORGE, a merchant from Montrose, a burgess of Arbroath, 1685. [ACB]
GRANT, GEORGE, a barber burgess of Arbroath, 1796. [AA. 18.941]
GRANT, JAMES, a burgess of Arbroath, 1674. [HHA]
GRANT, JAMES, a merchant in Arbroath, 1739; relict Margaret Dorward, testament, 1766, Comm. St Andrews. [NAS.AC8/590; AC9.1411]
GRANT, JAMES, a shoemaker in Arbroath, 1741. [AER.94]
GRANT, JAMES, a brewer in Arbroath, a Jacobite in 1745. [JA]
GRANT, JOHN, a burgess of Arbroath, father of Margaret, sasine, 1656. [NAS.RS35.S2.V.217][RGS.X.640; XI. 444]

GRANT, JOHN, in Millgait, Arbroath, 1658. [RGS.X.640]
GRANT, JOHN, hearth tax, Arbroath, 1691. [NAS.E69.11.1]
GRANT, JOHN, a merchant in Arbroath, 1734; treasurer of Arbroath, 1735; a merchant and sometime bailie of Arbroath, testament, 1749, Comm. St Andrews. [NAS.AC9.1311; CE70.1.2]
GRANT, MUNGO, a burgess of Arbroath, 1682. [ACB]
GRANT, WILLIAM, a merchant burgess of Arbroath, 1796. [AA.18.941]
GRAY, DAVID, in Dungeat, a burgess of Arbroath, 1690; a sasine, 1692. [ACB][NAS.RS35.S3.IX.136]; hearth tax, Arbroath, 1691. [NAS.E69.11.1]
GRAY, DAVID, a maltman in Arbroath, 1737, 1738, a Jacobite in 1745; relict Katherine Mather, testament, 1762, Comm. St Andrews. [NAS] [NAS.AC8/549, 565; AC10/314][JA]
GRAY, DAVID, a weaver in Arbroath, a Jacobite in 1745. [JA]
GRAY, JAMES, hearth tax, Arbirlot, 1691. [NAS.E69.11.1]
GRAY, JAN., in Muirden, Arbroath, 1752. [AER]
GRAY, ROBERT, in Carnoustie, a burgess of Arbroath, 1693. [ACB]
GRAY, THOMAS, a brewer and guilds-brother, husband of Isobel Grant, 1777. [Arbroath Abbey MI]
GRAY, WILLIAM, sheriff clerk of Forfar, was granted the lands of Kirkton of Aberbrothock, 24.7.1657. [RGS.X.605]
GRAY, WILLIAM, a tenant in Arbroath, 1658, 1663. [RGS.X.640; XI.444]
GRAY, WILLIAM, a burgess of Arbroath, 1798. [AA.18.941]
GREEN, EDWARD, in Montrose, a burgess of Arbroath, 1789. [AA.18.941]
GREGORY, ALESON, hearth tax, St Vigeans, 1691. [NAS.E69.11.1]
GREGORY, GEORGE, a skipper in Arbroath, deeds, 1687. [NAS.RD4.45/245]
GREGORY, JAMES, [1], a burgess of Arbroath, 1687. [ACB]
GREGORY, JAMES, [2], a burgess of Arbroath, 1693. [ACB]
GREGORIE, JAMES, hearth tax, Arbroath, 1691. [NAS.E69.11.1]
GREGORY, JAMES, hearth tax, St Vigeans, 1691. [NAS.E69.11.1]
GREGORIE, JOHN, a weaver in Arbroath, 1737. [AER.93]
GREIG, DAVID, a landowner in 1770; a merchant in Arbroath, Provost, 1797, husband of Magdalene Black,

(1739-1782), sasine. [Arbroath Abbey MI]
[NAS.RS35.24.122; GD45.16.278][DLS.26]
GREIG, JAMES, hearth tax, St Vigeans, 1691.
[NAS.E69.11.1]
GREIG, ROBERT, in Arbroath, 1687. [AA.A1.4.62]
GREIG, ROBERT, a weaver burgess of Arbroath, 1797. [AA.
18.941]
GREIG, WILLIAM, hearth tax, St Vigeans, 1691.
[NAS.E69.11.1]
GRIG, DAVID, hearth tax, Arbirlot, 1691. [NAS.E69.11.1]
GROOL, ALEXANDER, a skipper burgess of Arbroath, 1798.
[AA.18.941]
GUILD, GEORGE, a shoe-maker burgess of Arbroath, 1798.
[AA.18.941][Arbroath Abbey MI]
GUTHRIE, ALEXANDER, of Peebles near Arbroath, a
burgess of Arbroath, 1601. [HHA.138]
GUTHRIE, ALEXANDER, an Episcopal preacher and
Jacobite in Arbroath, 1715. [JA][HHA.170]
GUTHRIE, ANNA, hearth tax, Arbroath, 1691.
[NAS.E69.11.1]
GUTHRIE, BARBARA, in Almerie Close, Arbroath, 1752.
[AER]
GUTHRIE, DAVID, a burgess of Arbroath, husband of Agnes
Lindsay testament, 1598, Comm. St Andrews. [NAS]
GUTHRIE, Mr DAVID, a burgess of Arbroath, 1634.
[RGS.IX.1430]
GUTHRIE, DAVID, a skipper in Arbroath, 1661. [HHA.275]
GUTHRIE, DAVID, of Wester Seatoun, and his wife
Elizabeth, a sasine, 1676. [NAS.GD137.2465]
GUTHRIE, DAVID, of Carsebank, a burgess of Arbroath,
1686. [ACB]
GUTHRIE, DAVID, a tailor burgess of Arbroath, 1687; hearth
tax, Arbroath, 1691. [ACB][NAS.E69.11.1]
GUTHRIE, DAVID, a son of the burgh treasurer, a burgess of
Arbroath, 1684, father of David Guthrie, sasine, 1692.
[NAS.RS35.IX.546]
GUTHRIE, DAVID, hearth tax, Arbirlot, 1691.
[NAS.E69.11.1]
GUTHRIE, DAVID, a glover in Arbroath, 1730s. [AER.95]
GUTHRIE, Sir HENRY, of Kingedward, was served heir to
his grandfather Henry Grant of Colliston, a burgess of
Arbroath. [ACB][NAS.Retours. Forfar]

GUTHRIE, HENRY, hearth tax, Arbroath, 1691.
[NAS.E69.11.1]
GUTHRIE, HENRY, hearth tax, St Vigeans, 1691.
[NAS.E69.11.1]
GUTHRIE, ISABEL, co-heir to her grandfather Robert Guthrie of Kinblethmont, re land in Arbroath, 1675.
[NAS.Retours.Forfar]
GUTHRIE, JAMES, born 1590, son of Patrick Guthrie a goldsmith in St Andrews, graduated MA from St Andrews in 1610, minister at Arbirlot from 1625 to 1655, died 1662, husband of Isabella Durie in 1614, she died 1668, parents of James, John, and Jane. [F.5.421]
GUTHRIE, JAMES, in Arbroath, 1627. [RPCS.II.23]
GUTHRIE, JAMES, son of the treasurer, a burgess of Arbroath, 1684. [ACB]
GUTHRIE, JAMES, Dingwall Pursevant, a burgess of Arbroath, 1684. [ACB]
GUTHRIE, JAMES, a burgess of Arbroath, 1690. [ACB]
GUTHRIE, JANET, co-heir to her grandfather Robert Guthrie of Kinblethmont, re land in Arbroath, 1675; hearth tax, Arbroath, 1691. [NAS.E69.11.1; Retours.Forfar]
GUTHRIE, JEAN, co-heir to her grandfather Robert Guthrie of Kinblethmont, re land in Arbroath, 1675.
[NAS.Retours.Forfar]
GUTHRIE, JOHN, M.A., minister at Arbirlot from 1610 to 1617. [F.5.421]
GUTHRIE, JOHN, M.A., minister at Arbirlot from 1655 until 1667. [F.5.421]
GUTHRIE, JOHN, of Westhall, born in Arbirlot by Arbroath, 1664, son of Reverend John Guthrie and his wife Isabel Lamb, a merchant in Stockholm, Sweden. [F.5.319]
GUTHRIE, JOHN, a maltman burgess of Arbroath, 1683.
[ACB]
GUTHRIE, JOHN, son of the treasurer, a burgess of Arbroath, 1684. [ACB]
GUTHRIE, JOHN, a slater, hearth tax, Arbroath, 1691.
[NAS.E69.11.1]
GUTHRIE, JOHN, factor to the Earl of Southesk, admitted as a burgess of Arbroath in 1711. [NAS.GD45.15.43]
GUTHRIE, JOHN, a baker in Arbroath and co-owner of the St Thomas of Arbroath, 1743. [NAS.AC9.1500]

GUTHRIE, MARGARET, co-heir to her grandfather Robert Guthrie of Kinblethmont, re land in Arbroath, 1675. [NAS.Retours.Forfar]

GUTHRIE, PATRICK, of Auchmithie, a burgess of Arbroath, 1608. [RPCS.VIII.32]

GUTHRIE, WILLIAM, sometime in Kingary, a burgess of Arbroath, 1601. [ACB]

HADDON, JAMES, in Aberdeen, a burgess of Arbroath, 1791. [AA.18.941]

HADDON, JAMES, a burgess of Arbroath, 1794. [AA.18.941]

HAIG, WILLIAM, a merchant burgess of Arbroath, 1796. [AA.18.941]

HAILES, SAMUEL, a weaver in Arbroath, 1737. [AER.93]

HAILLS, DAVID, a baker burgess of Arbroath, husband of Geillis Fairer, testament, 1606, Comm. St Andrews. [NAS]

HAILLS, JOHN, a bailie burgess of Arbroath, 1599; depute bailie of the Regality of Arbroath, 1601. [HHA.138] [RGS.VI.1155]

HAILLS, JOHN, a mariner in Arbroath, 1611, [HHA.149]; master of the Grace of God of Arbroath, 1613. [ASW.73]

HAILLS, JOHN, a burgess of Arbroath, 1697. [ACB]

HAILLS, ROBERT, in Arbroath, 1687, 1693. [AA.A1.14.62/63]

HAILS, ROBERT, in Arbroath, a sasine,1733. [NAS.RS35.37, etc]

HALES, ALEXANDER, a merchant in Arbroath, born 1595, died 1630, husband of Eufame Grant. [Arbroath Abbey MI]

HALL, DAVID, a merchant in Arbroath, testament, 1709, Comm. St Andrews. [NAS]

HALL, HELEN, daughter of David Hall a merchant in Arbroath, testament, sasine,1784,Comm. St Andrews. [NAS. RS35.25.253]

HALS, ALEXANDER, hearth tax, Arbroath, 1691. [NAS.E69.11.1]

HAMILTON, AGNES, hearth tax, Arbroath, 1691. [NAS.E69.11.1]

HAMILTON, ARCHIBALD, a burgess of Arbroath, 1684. [ACB]

HAMILTON, ISABEL, hearth tax, Arbroath, 1691. [NAS.E69.11.1]

HAMILTON, JOHN, chamberlain of Arbroath, 1627, father of James Hamilton, both dead by 1657. [RPCS.II.23] [RGS.X.605]

HAMILTON, JOHN, a burgess of Arbroath, husband of Helen Peirson, father of Thomas Hamilton, sasine,1644. [NAS.RS335.SII.202]

HAMILTON, THOMAS, councillor of Arbroath, 1657, husband of Elspit Milne, testament, 1662, Comm. St Andrews. [NAS]

HANDASYDE, WILLIAM, a surgeon in Arbroath, son of John Handasyde, a merchant in Wooler formerly in Edinburgh, sasine, 1776. [NAS.RS35.25.509]

HASTINGS, ALEXANDER, a weaver burgess of Arbroath, 1797. [AA.18.941]

HASTON, WILLIAM, hearth tax, St Vigeans, 1691. [NAS.E69.11.1]

HAY, DAVID, master of the Margaret of Arbroath in 1682, and of the Christian of Arbroath 1684-1686, trading with Norway. [NAS.E72.16.6/14/15]

HAY, DAVID, hearth tax, Arbroath, 1691. [NAS.E69.11.1]

HAY, DAVID, in Berryfield, a burgess of Arbroath, 1687. [ACB]

HAY, DAVID, a weaver in Arbroath, admitted as a burgess of Arbroath,1763. [AA]

HAY, DAVID jr., a weaver in Arbroath, admitted as a burgess of Arbroath, 1797. [AA.X.101]

HAY, GEORGE, a burgess of Arbroath, 1688; hearth tax, Arbroath, 1691. [NAS.E69.11.1][ACB]

HAY, GEORGE, a skipper in Arbroath, relict Mary Gillespie, a sasine, 1765. [NAS.RS34.21.495]

HAY, JAMES, a merchant burgess of Arbroath, 1798. [AA. 18.941]

HAY, JOHN, hearth tax, Arbirlot, 1691. [NAS.E69.11.1]

HAY, JOHN, master of the Margaret of Arbroath, 1746, 1749, trading with Norway, Sweden, Danzig, and Holland; spouse Margaret Smith. [NAS.E504.24.1; E504.1.3] [AER.78]

HAY, Dr JOHN, in Grenada, a burgess of Arbroath, 1790. [AA.18.941]

HAY, JOHN, a tailor burgess of Arbroath, 1798. [AA.18.941]

HAY, WILLIAM, master of the John of Arbroath, trading with Norway, 1686. [NAS.E72.16.18]

HAY, WILLIAM, a tailor burgess of Arbroath, 1797. [AA. 18.941]

HAY, WILLIAM, a wright burgess of Arbroath, 1797. [AA. 18.941]

HEIR, DAVID, a skipper burgess of Arbroath, 1799. [AA. 18.941]

HEIR, WILLIAM, a weaver burgess of Arbroath, 1797. [AA. 18.941]

HENDERSON, ALEXANDER, born 1562, died 1652. [Arbirlot MI]

HENDERSON, ALEXANDER, hearth tax, Arbroath, 1691. [NAS.E69.11.1]

HENDERSON, ANDREW, a merchant burgess of Arbroath 1797. [AA.18.941]

HENDERSON, DAVID, a merchant burgess of Arbroath, 1797. [AA.18.941]

HENDERSON, HENDRY, in Arbroath, 1658. [RGS.X.640]

HENDERSON, JANET, hearth tax, Arbirlot, 1691. [NAS.E69.11.1]

HENDERSON, JOHN, hearth tax, St Vigeans, 1691. [NAS.E69.11.1]

HENDERSON, JOHN, a burgess of Arbroath, 1699. [ACB]

HENDERSON, JOHN, minister at St Vigeans from 1734 until 1753, husband of Anne Melville, parents of Margaret, Elizabeth, Robert, James, Jean, Alexander, Katherine, Amelia, and Williamina. [F.5.450]

HENDERSON, JOHN, a shoe-maker burgess of Arbroath, 1795. [AA.18.941]

HENDERSON, Sir JOHN, of Fordell, a burgess of Arbroath, 1790. [AA.18.941]

HENDERSON, ROBERT, a burgess of Arbroath, husband of Janet Lyn, a sasine, 1650. [NAS.RS35.S2.III.249]

HENNY, Dr JOHN, a physician in St Croix, West Indies, a burgess of Arbroath, 1791. [AA.18.941]

HENRY, CHARLES, a burgess of Arbroath, 1791. [AA. 18.941]

HENRY, ELIZABETH, in Almerie Close, Arbroath, 1752. [AER]

HENRYSON, WILLIAM, in Arbroath, 1658. [RGS.X.640]

HERCULESSON, ANDREW, from Arbroath, a citizen of Bergen, Norway, 16.. [SAB]

HERR, GEORGE, a weaver burgess of Arbroath, 1797. [AA. 18.941]

HEVI, JAMES, a weaver burgess of Arbroath, 1797. [AA. 18.941]
HEWSON, JAMES, in Lochlands, Arbroath, 1664. [NAS.GD45.16.1225]
HILL, DAVID, a mason burgess of Arbroath, 1797. [AA. 18.941]
HILL, GEORGE, a merchant in Arbroath, husband of Elizabeth Maule, parents of George who died 1780. [Arbroath Abbey MI]
HILL, HENRY, a burgess of Arbroath, 1683. [ACB]
HILL, JOHN, a flax-dresser burgess of Arbroath, 1797. [AA. 18.941]
HILL, ROBERT, a mason burgess of Arbroath, 1797. [AA. 18.941]
HILL, THOMAS, master of the John of Arbroath, trading with Norway, 1720s. [NAS.CE52.1.3; CE52.4.1]
HILL, WILLIAM, a burgess of Arbroath, 1606. [HHA.143]
HODGE, THOMAS, a weaver in Arbroath, 1766. [AER.93]
HOG, ROBERT, a weaver burgess of Arbroath, husband of Gells Simpson, testament, 1606, Comm. St Andrews. [NAS]
HOLDEN, ABRAHAM, a merchant in Arbroath, a sasine, 1761. [NAS.RS35.19.346, etc]
HOLDEN, DAVID, a merchant burgess of Arbroath, 1792. [AA.18.941]
HOLDEN, JOHN, a merchant burgess of Arbroath, 1792. [AA.18.941]
HOOD, JOHN, deacon of the shoemakers in Arbroath, 1680. [HHA.289]
HOOD, JOHN, [1], a burgess of Arbroath, 1688, hearth tax, Arbroath, 1691. [NAS.E69.11.1][ACB]
HOOD, JOHN, [2], burgess of Arbroath, 1689, hearth tax, Arbroath, 1691. [NAS.E69.11.1][ACB]
HOOM, WILLIAM, hearth tax, St Vigeans, 1691. [NAS.E69.11.1]
HOWDEN, ARTHUR, in Elsinore, Denmark, a burgess of Arbroath, 1790. [AA.18.941]
HUFFIN, WILLIAM, a weaver burgess of Arbroath, 1797. [AA.18.941]
HUMPHREYS, JOSHUA, late a hog-merchant in London, then residing in Arbroath, relict Elizabeth Campbell, testament, 1799, Comm. St Andrews. [NAS]

HUNTER, ALEXANDER, a seaman in Arbroath, testament, 1724, Comm. St Andrews. [NAS]

HUNTER, DAVID, a burgess of Arbroath, husband of Anna Mackoule, a sasine, 1642. [NAS.RS35.S2.II.104]

HUNTER, DAVID, in Arbroath, husband of Margaret Anderson, testament, 1692, Comm. St Andrews. [NAS]

HUNTER, GEORGE, in Fairnieknowe, a burgess of Arbroath, 1681. [ACB]

HUNTER, HENRY, born 1717 son of David Hunter and his wife Jean Watt, in Newton Arbirlot, a Jacobite in 1745. [JA]

HUNTER, JAMES, council post [man], a burgess of Arbroath, 1688. [ACB]

HUNTER, JAMES, a merchant in Arbroath, 1738. [NAS.AC8/565]

HUNTER, JAMES, a bailie of Arbroath, 1753. [NAS.E326.1.133]

HUNTER, JAMES, a weaver burgess of Arbroath, 1789. [AA.18.941]

HUNTER, JAMES, in St Andrews, a burgess of Arbroath, 1789. [AA.18.941]

HUNTER, JOHN, in Newton Arbirlot, a Jacobite in 1745. [JA]

HUNTER, JOHN, a Professor in St Andrews, a burgess of Arbroath, 1789. [AA.18.941]

HUNTER, PATRICK, hearth tax, Arbirlot, 1691. [NAS.E69.11.1]

HUNTER, PATRICK, a burgess of Arbroath, 1695. [ACB]

HUNTER, ROBERT, a burgess of Arbroath, 1687.[ACB]

HUNTER, THOMAS, minister at Arbirlot from 1759 until his death in 1789, husband of Marjory Charteris, parents of William, Thomas, and Charles. [F.5.421]

HUNTER, WILLIAM, hearth tax, Arbroath, 1691. [NAS.E69.11.1]

HUNTER, WILLIAM, a carrier burgess of Arbroath, 1794. [AA.18.941]

HUSBAND, JAMES, a merchant burgess of Arbroath, 1794. [AA.18.941]

HUSSEY, JAMES, wright in Bonnyton, Arbirlot, died aged 70, married in 1776 to Elizabeth Ferrier, born 1745, died 1815, daughter Elizabeth, born 1778, died 1816. [Arbirlot MI]

HUTCHEON, ALEXANDER, a flesher burgess of Arbroath, 1794. [AA.18.941]

HUTCHEON, JOHN, Provost of Arbroath, 1693; 1727. [AA.A1.1463][NAS.CS271.47511]

HUTCHESON, DAVID, hearth tax, Arbroath, 1691. [NAS.E69.11.1]

HUTCHISON, JOHN, a merchant and late Provost of Arbroath, a Jacobite imprisoned in Edinburgh and Carlisle.1711, 1716, escaped to Bordeaux, France. [NAS.AC9.23M2; AC13.1.163][JA] [TNA.SP54.12.147]

HUTCHISON, ROBERT, born 1699, died 1773. [St Vigeans MI]

INGLIS, ALEXANDER, graduated MA from St Andrews in 1587, minister at St Vigeans from 1622 to 1645, father of Peter Inglis. [F.5.449]

INGLIS, ..., master of the Two Sisters of Arbroath, trading with Bordeaux, France,1751. [AJ.163/165]

INGLIS, JAMES, of Peebles, by Arbroath, a shipmaster in Arbroath, spouse of Martha Spink, 1753. [AER.80]

INGLIS, JOHN, master of the John of Arbroath, trading with Norway, 1720s. [NAS.CE52.1.3;CE52.4.1]

INGLIS, Mr PATRICK, hearth tax, Arbroath, 1691. [NAS.E69.11.1]

INNES, GEORGE, a burgess of Arbroath, 1687. [ACB]

INNES, Mr LEWIS, Rector of the Scots College in Paris, a burgess of Arbroath, 1687. [ACB]

INTRIE, JOHN, hearth tax, Arbroath, 1691. [NAS.E69.11.1]

IRELAND, JOHN, a book-seller burgess of Arbroath, 1797. [AA.18.941]

IRINSIE, Major NINIAN, a burgess of Arbroath, 1795. [AA.18.941]

IRVINE, ROBERT, a shoe-maker burgess of Arbroath, 1798. [AA.18.941]

IRVING, JAMES, minister of Arbirlot from 1617 until his death in 1625, husband of Helen Strachan, father of Alexander Irving. [F.5.421]

JACK, JOHN, born 1757, a skipper in Arbroath, died 1801, husband of Jean Brown. [Arbroath Abbey MI]

JACK, JOHN, a weaver burgess of Arbroath, 1797. [AA.18.941]

JACK, ROBERT, master of the Christian of Arbroath, trading with Norway in 1686. [NAS.E72.16.18]

JAFFRESON, JAMES, hearth tax, Arbroath, 1691.
[NAS.E69.11.1]
JAMESON, ALEXANDER, hearth tax, Arbroath, 1691.
[NAS.E69.11.1]
JAMIE, JOHN, a mason in Arbroath, a sasine, 1778.
[NAS.RS35.27.42]
JAMIESON, ALEXANDER, a burgess of Arbroath, 1693.
[ACB]
JAMIESON, JAMES, a burgess of Arbroath, testament, 1693, Comm. St Andrews. [NAS]
JARRON, DAVID, a hay-dresser burgess of Arbroath, 1797.
[AA.18.941]
JARVIS, ROBERT, a merchant burgess of Arbroath, 1792.
[AA.18.941]
JAY, JOHN, a merchant in Rotterdam, Netherlands, a burgess of Arbroath, 1791. [AA.18.941]
JOHNSTON, ALEXANDER, hearth tax, Arbirlot, 1691.
[NAS.E69.11.1]
JOHNSTON, CHARLES, a wright burgess of Arbroath, 1791.
[AA.18.941]
JOHNSTON or SOUTAR, DAVID, of Wardmilne, 1663.
[HHA.157]
JOHNSTON, DAVID, a weaver in Arbroath, 1748. [AER.93]
JOHNSTON, GEORGE, a wright burgess of Arbroath, 1797.
[AA.18.941]
JOHNSTON, JAMES, hearth tax, Arbirlot, 1691.
[NAS.E69.11.1]
JOHNSTON, JAMES, a burgess of Arbroath, his relict Elspeth Duncan, testament, 1687, Comm. St Andrews.
[NAS]
JOHNSTONE, JAMES, born 1626, treasurer of Arbroath, died 1685. [Arbroath Abbey MI]
JOHNSTON, JAMES, a weaver in Arbroath, 1737. [AER.93]
JOHNSTON, JAMES, born 1731, died 29 October 1806, linen manufacturer and Provost, husband of Ann Anderson (1738-1786); 1758. [NAS.E326.1.133] [Arbroath Abbey MI]
JOHNSTON, JOHN, hearth tax, Arbirlot, 1691.
[NAS.E69.11.1]
JOHNSTON, JOHN, in Crudie, a burgess of Arbroath, 1790.
[AA.18.941]
JOHNSTON, THOMAS, hearth tax, Arbirlot, 1691.
[NAS.E69.11.1]

JOHNSTON, WILLIAM, husband of Janet Millar, parents of Jean born 1715, died 1717. [Arbirlot MI]
JOLLY, DAVID, a merchant in Arbroath, spouse Margaret Gardner, sasine, 1771. [NAS.RS35.23.258]
JUSTIN, ANDREW, hearth tax, Arbirlot, 1691. [NAS.E69.11.1]
KAY, HENDRIE, a shoemaker in Arbroath, 1737, deacon in 1741, and an officer of the craft in 1755. [AER.94]
KAY, JAMES, a weaver in Arbroath, 1742. [AER.93]
KAY, JAMES, a shoemaker in Arbroath, 1737. [AER.94]
KAY, JOHN, hearth tax, Arbirlot, 1691. [NAS.E69.11.1]
KAY, JOHN, a shoemaker in Arbroath, 1739. [AER.94]
KEILL, DAVID, hearth tax, Arbirlot, 1691. [NAS.E69.11.1]
KEILL, JAMES, born 1733, a gunner in the Royal Navy, husband of Elizabeth Cargill, died 1816. [Arbroath Abbey MI]
KEITH, ALEXANDER, a merchant and Provost of Arbroath, sasine,1760. [NAS.RS35.19.273]
KEITH, ALEXANDER, a tailor burgess of Arbroath, 1791. [AA.18.941]
KEITH, DAVID, born 1758, a skipper in Arbroath in 1778, died 1821. [NAS.S/H][Arbroath Abbey MI]
KEIR, GEORGE, a burgess of Arbroath, 1791. [AA.18.941]
KEITH, ALEXANDER, a merchant in Arbroath, co-owner of the St Thomas of Arbroath, 1743, 1745; merchant and late provost of Arbroath, testament, 1774,Comm. St Andrews. [NAS.AC9.1500, 1669; AC10/314; GD45.18.2439]
KELLIE, JOHN, a skipper of Arbroath, in Aberdeen, 1610. [ASW.58]
KENNEDY, JOHN, shoremaster of Arbroath, a letter, 1712. [NAS.E230.3.2]
KENNY, ALEXANDER, a skipper in Arbroath, 1717. [NAS.AC9.616]
KENNY, CHARLES, a carpenter and former treasurer of Arbroath, spouse Katrin Spink, sasine; a bailie in Arbroath, testament, 1719, Comm. St Andrews. [NAS. RS35.12.349]
KENNY, CHARLES, born 1707, master of the John and David of Arbroath, trading with Danzig, Riga, Norway and Spain in the 1740s, of the Industry of Arbroath, 1767, of the Owners Goodwill of Arbroath, 1768, died

1785, husband of Mathilda Miln. [NAS.AC11.162; E504.24.1/2; CE53.1.5/7][Arbroath Abbey MI]

KENNY, CHARLES, a mariner in Arbroath, testament, 1803, Comm. St Andrews. [NAS]

KENNY, GEORGE, sometime a carpenter burgess of Arbroath, relict Janet Kinneares, testament, 1706, Comm. St Andrews. [NAS]

KENNY, JANET, spouse of James Forsyth in Arbroath, testament, 1616, Comm. Brechin. [NAS]

KENNY, JOHN, master of a 90 ton boat of Arbroath, 1725. [NAS.AC9.945]

KENNY, JOHN, a ships carpenter in Arbroath, sasine, 1767. [NAS.RS35.22.392]; dead by 1753. [AER.69]

KENNY, WILLIAM, master of the Two Brothers of Arbroath, the Margaret of Arbroath, the John and David of Arbroath, trading with Norway, Riga, Germany, and Sweden, in the1740s, and the Margaret and Mary of Arbroath, 1749, trading with Rotterdam, 1746; husband of Katherine Gillespie, sasine. [NAS.E504.24.1/2; AC8/717; CE53.1.4; RS35.21.495] [AJ#259]

KERRIE, ALEXANDER, a sailor in Arbroath, a Jacobite in1745. [JA]

KERRIE, JOHN, a merchant in Arbroath, a Jacobite in 1745. [JA]

KEY, JOHN, hearth tax, Arbroath, 1691 deacon of the tailors of Arbroath, husband of Elizabeth Rainy (1690-1731). [Arbroath Abbey MI][JA][NAS.E69.11.1]

KEY, PETER, born 1761, a skipper in Arbroath, husband of Jean Hackney, died 1813. [Arbroath Abbey MI]

KEY, THOMAS, hearth tax, Arbroath, 1691. [NAS.E69.11.1]

KEY, WILLIAM, a burgess of Arbroath, 1697. [ACB]

KIDD, ALEXANDER, hearth tax, St Vigeans, 1691. [NAS.E69.11.1]

KIDD, DAVID, hearth tax, Arbroath, 1691. [NAS.E69.11.1]

KIDD, Captain GEORGE, in Arbroath, 1753. [NAS.E326.1.133]

KIDD, GEORGE, a merchant and late bailie in Arbroath, sasine,1773. [NAS.RS35.24.119]

KID, GEORGE, born 1739, a skipper in Arbroath, died 1829, husband of Agnes Alexander. [Arbroath Abbey MI]

KIDD, JAMES, a schoolmaster in Arbroath, a Jacobite in 1715. [JA]

KID, JOHN, bailie of Arbroath, 1681; provost of Arbroath, deeds,1687. [RPCS.XIII.xx][HHA.157] [NAS.RD3.69.720; RD2.69.54]

KINARIES, CIRSTEN, hearth tax, Arbroath, 1691. [NAS.E69.11.1]

KINNEAR, ANDREW, in Arbroath, 1664. [NAS.GD45.16.1225]

KINNEAR, CHRISTIAN, wife of John Murison a merchant in Arbroath, 1702. [AA.A1.14.64]

KINNEAR, HENRY, a burgess of Arbroath, wife Bessie Caird, testament, 1616, Comm. St Andrews. [NAS]

KINNEAR, JAMES, master of the bark Elizabeth of Arbroath, 1722. [NAS.AC8/279]

KINNEAR, THOMAS, master of the Concord of Arbroath, trading with Riga in 1746. [NAS.E504.11.1]

KINNIE, DAVID, hearth tax, Arbirlot, 1691. [NAS.E69.11.1]

KNIGHT, WILLIAM, a sawyer burgess of Arbroath, 1799. [AA.18.941]

KNOX, ALEXANDER, a servant to Thomas Renny, a burgess of Arbroath, 1789. [AA.18.941]

KORD, ALEXANDER, hearth tax, St Vigeans, 1691. [NAS.E69.11.1]

KYD, ALEXANDER, a burgess of Arbroath, 1688, councillor in Arbroath, 16.. [HHA][ACB]

KYD, ALEXANDER, a shoemaker in Arbroath, 1745. [AER.94]

KYD, DAVID, a burgess of Arbroath, 1683. [ACB]

KYD, DAVID, son of James Kyd, an apprentice glover in 1735, a master glover in 1745. [AER.95]

KYD, GEORGE, a burgess of Arbroath, 1688. [ACB]

KYD, GEORGE, a merchant in Arbroath, 1768. [NAS.AD58.345]

KYD, GEORGE, a weaver burgess of Arbroath, 1797. [AA.18.941]

KYD, JAMES, a burgess of Arbroath, 1688. [ACB]

KYD, JAMES, of Craigie, parish of Arbroath, relict Helen Fotheringham, testament, 1746, Comm. St Andrews. [NAS]

KYD, JAMES, deacon of the glover craft of Arbroath 1735. [AER.95]

KYD, JAMES, a weaver in Arbroath, 1764. [AER.93]

KYD, JOHN, born 1641, died 1694, a burgess of Arbroath, 1688. [ACB][Arbroath Abbey MI]

KYD, THOMAS, in Carmyllie, a burgess of Arbroath, 1681. [ACB]
KYDE, WILLIAM, a merchant burgess of Arbroath, 1796. [AA.18.941]
LAING, MARGARET, spouse of William Matthew in Arbroath, testament, 1674, Comm. St Andrews. [NAS]
LAINGYARDS, JAMES, a heckler burgess of Arbroath, 1797. [AA.18.941]
LAIRD, Captain DAVID, a burgess of Arbroath, 1795. [AA.18.941]
LAMB, ALEXANDER, in Arbroath, 1664. [NAS.GD45.16.1225]
LAMB, ANDREW, a tenant in Arbroath, 1663. [RGS.XI.444]
LAMB, DAVID, hearth tax, Arbroath, 1691. [NAS.E69.11.1]
LAMB, DAVID, hearth tax, St Vigeans, 1691. [NAS.E69.11.1]
LAMB, DAVID, in Berryfauld, Arbroath, 1752. [AER]
LAMB, JAMES, in South Tarry, a burgess of Arbroath, 1601. [HHA.138]
LAMB, JAMES, in Seagait, Arbroath, 1658. [RGS.X.640]
LAMB, JAMES, son of Andrew Lamb of Tarry, a burgess of Arbroath, 1685. [ACB]
LAMB, JAMES, hearth tax, St Vigeans, 1691. [NAS.E69.11.1]
LAMB, JAMES, a merchant in Arbroath, 1793. [NAS.CS234.SEQN.L.1.14]
LAMB, JOHN, hearth tax, Arbroath, 1691. [NAS.E69.11.1]
LAMB, JOHN, hearth tax, Arbirlot, 1691. [NAS.E69.11.1]
LAMB, JOHN, tenant of land in Dishland, Arbroath, 1716. [NAS.E650/2]
LAMB, JOHN, a weaver in Arbroath, 1765. [AER.93]
LAMB, JON., in Almerie Close, Arbroath, 1752. [AER]
LANIGAN, JAMES, a manufacturer burgess of Arbroath, 1796. [AA.18.941]
LAUDER, MARGARET, wife of David Wichton a maltman burgess of Arbroath, testament, 1617, Comm. St Andrews. [NAS]
LAURENCE, JAMES, hearth tax, St Vigeans, 1691; beadle of St Vigeans, a Jacobite in 1715, deposed. [NAS.E69.11.1; CH2.15.3][HHA.170]
LAURENCE, PATRICK, hearth tax, Arbirlot, 1691. [NAS.E69.11.1]
LAW, JAMES, a maltman in Arbroath, 1610. [HHA.148]

LAW, JOHN, master of the Seaflower of Arbroath, trading with Mulde, Norway, 1750. [AJ.149]
LAWSON, KATHERINE, born 1641, died 1676, wife of Patrick Smith. [Arbirlot MI]
LAWSON, JAMES, master of a 10 ton boat of Arbroath, 1725. [NAS.AC9.945]
LAWSON, JOHN, sr., a lobster fisher in Arbroath, 1768. [NAS.CE53.1.6]
LAWSON, JOHN, jr., a lobster fisher in Arbroath, 1768. [NAS.CE53.1.6]
LAWSON, PATRICK, master of the Ann of Arbroath, 1716; master of a 12 ton boat, 1725. [NAS.AC9.567, 945]
LECKIE, DAVID, a smith burgess of Arbroath, 1790. [AA.18.941]
LEPER, JAMES, born 1633, a hammerman burgess, died 1677, wife Jean Leslie, born 1624, died 1700. [St Vigeans MI]
LEIPER, JAMES, a smith in Arbroath, sasine,1711. [NAS.RS35.12.221]
LEIPER, JOHN, a smith in Arbroath, sasine, 1711. [NAS.RS35.12.221]
LEITCH, THOMAS, in Arbroath, testament, 1747, Comm. St Andrews. [NAS]
LESLIE, ALEXANDER, a weaver burgess of Arbroath, 1797. [AA.18.941]
LESLIE, ANDREW, a shoemaker in Arbroath 1750s, husband of Margaret Allan, sasine,1771. [AER.94] [NAS.RS35.XXIII.268]
LESLIE, GEORGE, hearth tax, St Vigeans, 1691. [NAS.E69.11.1]
LESLIE, HENRY, hearth tax, Arbroath, 1691. [NAS.E69.11.1]
LESLIE, JOHN, a burgess of Arbroath, 1686; hearth tax, Arbroath, 1691. [NAS.E69.11.1] [ACB]
LESLIE, JOHN, hearth tax, St Vigeans, 1691.[NAS.E69.11.1]
LESLIE, ROBERT, of South Tarry, a Justice of the Peace in 1686, hearth tax, St Vigeans, 1691. [NAS.E69.11.1] [RPCS.XI.574]
LESLIE, THOMAS, hearth tax, St Vigeans, 1691. [NAS.E69.11.1]
LEUCHARS, JAMES, hearth tax, St Vigeans, 1691. [NAS.E69.11.1]
LEYS, THOMAS, a burgess of Arbroath, 1797. [AA.18.941]

LIDDELL, DAVID, a smith, hearth tax, Arbroath, 1691.
[NAS.E69.11.1]

LIDDEL, GEORGE, a burgess of Arbroath, 1595; 1601.
[NAS.Cal.Deeds.49.169][RGS.6.1197]

LIGHTON, JAMES, a burgess and guildsbrother of Arbroath, spouse of Margaret Vannet, 1796. [Arbroath Abbey MI]

LIGHTON, JOHN, in Dunninald, a burgess of Arbroath, 1792. [AA.18.941]

LIGHTON, GEORGE, a merchant burgess of Arbroath, 1795.

LILLIE, WILLIAM, a gardener in Arbroath, sasine, 1768.
[NAS.RS35.XXII.445]

LIN, WILLIAM, master of the Gift of God of Arbroath, in aAberdeen, 1612. [ASW.73]

LINDORES, Lord JOHN, a burgess of Arbroath, 1682.
[ACB]

LINDSAY, AGNES, wife of David Guthrie a burgess of Arbroath, testament, 1598, Comm. St Andrews. [NAS]

LINDSAY, ALEXANDER, a merchant in Arbroath, 1736.
[AER.95]

LINDSAY, DAVID, of Edzell, a burgess of Arbroath, 1686.
[NAS]

LINDSAY, HELEN, wife of James Stevenson a burgess of Arbroath, testament, 1606, Comm. St Andrews. [NAS]

LINDSAY, JAMES, a gunsmith burgess of Arbroath, 1694.
[ACB]

LINDSAY, JAMES, a bailie of Arbroath, 1725.
[NAS.GD3.14.2.1.54]

LINDSAY, JOHN, a shoemaker burgess of Arbroath, 1797.
[AA.18.941]

LINDSAY, PATRICK, of Kirkton, M.A., minister at St Vigeans from 1593 and 1613. [F.5.449]

LITTLEJOHN, ALEXANDER, hearth tax, Arbroath, 1691.
[NAS.E69.11.1]

LITTLEJOHN, ALEXANDER, a skipper in Arbroath, master of the Wallace and Gardyne, trading with Riga, 1770s, husband of Isabel Wallace, sasine. [NAS.RS35.24.317; CE53.1.8]

LITTLEJOHN, ALEXANDER, a tailor burgess of Arbroath, 1790. [AA.18.941]

LITTLEJOHN, ALEXANDER, a weaver burgess of Arbroath, 1797. [AA.18.941]

LITTLEJOHN, ELSPIT, hearth tax, Arbroath, 1691.
[NAS.E69.11.1]

LITTLEJOHN, JAMES, hearth tax, Arbroath, 1691; a burgess of Arbroath, 1696. [ACB] [NAS.E69.11.1]
LITTLEJOHN, JAMES, a flax-dresser burgess of Arbroath, 1797. [AA.18.941]
LITTLEJOHN, JOHN, hearth tax, St Vigeans, 1691. [NAS.E69.11.1]
LITTLEJOHN, JOHN, a burgess and ground-labourer in Millgait, Arbroath, born 1698, died 6 November 1741. [Arbroath Abbey MI]
LITTLEJOHN, KATHERINE, in Arbroath, testament, 1746, Comm. St Andrews. [NAS]
LITTLEJOHN, THOMAS, hearth tax, Arbroath, 1691. [NAS.E69.11.1]
LITTLEJOHN, WILLIAM, a weaver burgess of Arbroath, 1686. [ACB]
LITTLEJOHN, WILLIAM, a shoemaker burgess of Arbroath, 1797. [AA.18.941]
LIVINGSTONE, ..., of Dunlappie, a burgess of Arbroath, 1684. [NAS]
LOGIE, ALEXANDER, hearth tax, Arbroath, 1691. [NAS.E69.11.1]
LOGIE, BARNARD, a burgess of Arbroath, testament, 1619, Comm. St Andrews. [NAS]
LOGGIE, JAMES, hearth tax, Arbroath, 1691. [NAS.E69.11.1]
LOUSON, JAMES, hearth tax, Arbirlot, 1691. [NAS.E69.11.1]
LOUSON, JAMES, a merchant burgess of Arbroath, born 1715, died 11 December 1779, husband of Agnes Thomson. [Arbroath Abbey MI]; a merchant in Arbroath, 1738; 1742. [AER.95][NAS.AC9.1479]
LOUSON, JOHN, hearth tax, St Vigeans, 1691. [NAS.E69.11.1]
LOUSON, JOHN, a burgess of Arbroath, 1683. [ACB]
LOUSON, JOHN, hearth tax, Arbroath, 1691. [NAS.E69.11.1]
LOW, AGNES, hearth tax, Arbroath, 1691. [NAS.E69.11.1]
LOW, ANDREW, a slater burgess of Arbroath, testament, 1662, Comm. St Andrews. [NAS]
LOW, ANDREW, master of the Magdalene of Arbroath, 1740s trading with Danzig, Norway, and Portugal; trading with Norway 1752. [NAS.E504.24.1/2; E504.1.2][AJ.219]

LOW, DAVID, master of the Magdalene of Arbroath, 1740s, trading with Riga, Ireland and Sweden. [NAS.E504.24.1/2]

LOW, HERCULES, master of a 18 ton boat of Arbroath, 1725; master of the Isobell of Arbroath, trading with Norway,1742-1743; and of the Magdalene of Arbroath, 1744-1746, trading with Norway. [NAS.AC9.945; E504.24.1; E504.1.1]

LOW, JOHN, master of the Seaflower of Arbroath, trading with Germany, Sweden, Norway, Holland, Portugal and Riga, 1740s. [NAS.E504.24.1/2]

LOWPAR, JOHN, a blacksmith in Arbroath, a Jacobite in1745. [JA]

LUMGAIR, ANDREW, a burgess of Arbroath, 1684. [ACB]

LUMGAIR, JOHN, hearth tax, Arbroath, 1691. [NAS.E69.11.1]

LUMGAIR, WILLIAM, hearth tax, Arbirlot, 1691. [NAS.E69.11.1]

LUNDIE, JOHN, hearth tax, St Vigeans, 1691. [NAS.E69.11.1]

LUNDIE, WILLIAM, in Arbroath, testament, 1687, Comm. St Andrews. [NAS]

LYELL, ANDREW, hearth tax, Arbirlot, 1691. [NAS.E69.11.1]

LYELL, CHARLES, a burgess of Arbroath, 1793. [AA. 18.941]

LYELL, DAVID, a burgess and clerk of Arbroath, 1649. [RGS.XI.2136]

LYELL, DAVID, a burgess of Arbroath, 1698. [ACB]

LYELL, JAMES, a merchant burgess of Arbroath, 1684; heir to his father Arthur Lyell a merchant in Edinburgh, 1685. [NAS.Retours, Edinburgh]

LYALL, JAMES, in Arbroath, 1753. [NAS.E326.1.133]

LYELL, JOHN, deacon convenor of Arbroath, 1681. [HHA. 157]

LYALL, JOHN, a burgess of Arbroath, 1691; hearth tax, Arbroath, 1691. [NAS.E69.11.1][ACB]

LYELL, JOHN, hearth tax, Arbroath, 1691. [NAS.E69.11.1]

LYELL, JOHN, hearth tax, St Vigeans, 1691. [NAS.E69.11.1]

LYELL, MATTHEW, a tailor in Arbroath, admitted as a burgess and freeman of Arbroath in 1758. [AA.X.102]

LYELL, PATRICK, a merchant in Arbroath, heir to his father Patrick Lyell in Guthrie, 1685. [NAS.Retours. Forfar]

LYELL, ROBERT, treasurer of Arbroath, 1611. [HHA. 147/194]

LYELL, STEWART, formerly a merchant in Arbroath, son of Thomas Lyell the elder of Gardyne, spouse Janet Gairdner, sasine,1756; landowner of Dickmontlaw, Newgait, and part of Ponderlaw, 1770. [NAS.RS35.18.132, etc][DLS.26]

LYELL, THOMAS, the younger of Gardyne, admitted as a burgess of Arbroath in 1735. [NAS.NRAS#0056]

LYELL, THOMAS, of Gardyne, parish of Arbroath, testament, 1793, Comm. St Andrews. [NAS]

LYNE, JOHN, a burgess of Arbroath, dead by 1633. [NAS.Retours.Forfar]

LYNE, ROBERT, a burgess of Arbroath, 1608; a councillor in 1617. [RPCS.8.33][HHA.150]

LYNE, WILLIAM, a burgess of Arbroath, heir to his grandfather John Lyne a burgess of Arbroath, 1632. [NAS.Retours.Forfar]

LYON, PATRICK, of Carnoustie, a burgess of Arbroath, 1687. [ACB]

MACHANE, JOHN, a seaman in Auchmithie, testament, 1614, St Andrews. [NAS]

MCCOULL, JOHN, a burgess of Arbroath, and daughters Anna and Margaret, a sasine, 1642. [NAS.RS35.S2.II.104]

MCDONALD, JAMES, a weaver burgess of Arbroath, 1797. [AA.18.941]

MCDONALD, JOHN, a mason burgess of Arbroath, 1798. [AA.18.941]

MCGHIE, JOHN, an Excise officer and a burgess of Arbroath, 1794. [AA.18.941]

MAKGILL, GEORGE, born 1641, son of Patrick Makgill minister at Monikie, MA St Andrews 1662, minister at Arbirlot from 1667, husband of Margaret Guthrie, parents of Alexander Makgill. [F.5.421]

MCGILL, Mr GEORGE, a writer in Edinburgh, a burgess of Arbroath, 1699. [ACB]

MACKIE, ALEXANDER, born 1732, son of Reverend James Mackie, minister at Arbroath from 1766 until 1787, husband of Mary Pearson. [F.5.425]

MACKIE, ALEXANDER, in Arbroath, a Jacobite in 1745. [JA]

MCGRANE, MICHAEL, in Bordeaux, France, a burgess of Arbroath, 1791. [AA.18.941]

MCINTOSH, GEORGE, a wright burgess of Arbroath, 1797. [AA.18.941]

MCINTOSH, JOHN, a bookbinder burgess of Arbroath, 1797. [AA.18.941]

MCKAY, DONALD, a mason burgess of Arbroath, 1798. [AA.18.941]

MCKENZIE, DUNCAN, a burgess of Arbroath, 1699. [ACB]

MCKIE, ALEXANDER, a burgess of Arbroath, 1684, hearth tax, 1691. [ACB][NAS.E69.11.1]

MACKIE, ALEXANDER, born 1722, son of James Mackie, minister at Arbroath from 1776 until 1787, husband of Mary Pearson. [F.5.425]

MACKIE, ALEXANDER, in Arbroath, 1745. [JA]

MACKIE, JAMES, hearth tax, Arbroath, 1691. [NAS.E69.11.1]

MCKIESON, PATRICK, in Lochlands, Arbroath, 1658. [RGS.X.640]

MCNICOLL, ALEXANDER, servant to the Ear of Northesk, a burgess of Arbroath, 1693. [ACB]

MCPHERSON, ARCHIBALD, of Auchmithie, Justice of the Peace in Arbroath, 1686. [RPCS.XI.574]

MADER, JOHN, a maltman in Arbroath, hearth tax,1691; a burgess of Arbroath, 1698. [NAS.E69.11.1][ACB]

MAIRS, ALEXANDER, a dyer burgess of Arbroath, 1797. [AA.18.941]

MANN, ALEXANDER, a weaver burgess of Arbroath, 1797. [AA.18.941]

MAN, JOHN, a maltman, hearth tax, Arbroath, 1691. [NAS.E69.11.1]

MANN, JOHN, a merchant in Arbroath, 1744. [NAS.AC11.162]

MAR, JAMES, a chpaman burgess of Arbroath, husband of Helen Duncan, testament, 1600, Comm. St Andrews. [NAS]

MARCHAR, JOHN, a skipper of Arbroath, in Aberdeen, 1610. [ASW.60]

MARNIE, DAVID, a shoemaker in Arbroath, 1766; a burgess of Arbroath, 1791. [AA.18.941][AER.94]

MARNIE, JAMES, [AA.18.941]; born 1776, died 12 March 1849, Provost, husband of Mary Auchterlony, (1773-1856). [Arbroath Abbey MI]

MARR, JAMES, son of deacon John Marr, an apprentice glover in 1736. [AER.95]

MARTIN, Lieutenant ROBERT, a burgess of Arbroath, 1795. [AA.18.941]

MARTIN, TOBIAS, educated at Glasgow University, minister at St Vigeans from 1727 until 1730. [F.5.450]

MASSIE, JOHN, a Sergeant of Captain Murray's Company of Colonel Row's Regiment, a burgess of Arbroath, 1699. [ACB]

MATHER, JOHN, a weaver in Arbroath 1738, spouse Jean Peddie, a sasine, 1736. [NAS.RS35.15.339][AER.93]

MATHIE, WILLIAM, hearth tax, Arbroath, 1691. [NAS.E69.11.1]

MATTHEW, ANDREW, a weaver burgess of Arbroath, 1797. [AA.18.941]

MATTHEW, WALTER, a burgess of Arbroath, 1797. [AA.18.941]

MATHIE, JAMES, hearth tax, Arbroath, 1691. [NAS.E69.11.1]

MAULE, Mr GEORGE, factor to the Earl of Panmure, a burgess of Arbroath, 1693. [ACB]

MAULE, Mr HARRY, of Kelly, son of George Maule the Earl of Panmure, hearth tax, Arbirlot, 1691; a burgess of Arbroath in 1713; a Jacobite in 1715, fought at Sheriffmuir, escaped to the Netherlands, died in 1734. [NAS.E69.11.1; GD45.15.44][SP.VII.26]

MAULE, HENRY, a merchant in Arbroath, 1729. [NAS.AC9.1083]

MAULE, JAMES, hearth tax, Arbirlot, 1691. [NAS.E69.11.1]

MAULE, JAMES, an MD in Arbroath, son of George Maule in Boath, sasine, 1717. [NAS.RS35.13.183, etc]

MEARNS, ALEXANDER, a merchant in Arbroath, a deed, 1697. [NAS.RD3.87.554]

MEEKISON, AGNES, heir to her father James Meekison a dyer burgess of Dundee, to the lands of Dishland and Keptie in Arbroath, 1676; tenant of land in Dishland, Arbroath, 1716. [NAS.Retours.Forfar; E650/2]

MEIKESON, DAVID, a shoe-maker in Arbroath, 1768. [AER.94]

MEIKESON, JAMES, a shoe-maker in Arbroath, 1740. [AER.94]

MEEKISON, PATRICK, a burgess of Arbroath, and his spouse Isobel Carnegy, a sasine, 1664. [NAS.RS35.S3.II.251]
MEEKISON, WILLIAM, a burgess of Arbroath, 1699. [ACB]
MEIKISON, CHARLES, a mariner in Arbroath, died 1749, testament, 1755, Comm. St Andrews. [NAS][AER.84]
MEIKISON, JOHN, a burgess of Arbroath, 1696. [BA]
MELESS, GEORGE, a merchant from Perth, and a burgess of Arbroath, 1790. [AA.18.941]
MELVILLE, JOHN, a burgess of Arbroath, 1608. [RGS.6.2117]
METHVEN, JOHN, deacon of the wrights in Arbroath, 1680. [HHA.289]
MICKIESON, PATRICK, hearth tax, Arbroath, 1691. [NAS.E69.11.1]
MIDDLETON, DAVID, a merchant burgess of Arbroath, 1798. [AA.18.941]
MIDDLETON, JOHN, servant to the Earl of Panmure, a burgess of Arbroath, 1696. [ACB]
MIKESON, JOHN, born 1631, a maltman burgess of Arbroath in 1687, died 1694, spouse Agnes Shakirt, born 1644, died 1703. [Arbroath Abbey MI]
MIKESON, WILLIAM, in Boathloaning, a burgess of Arbroath, 1681. [ACB]
MILISON, ANDREW, hearth tax, St Vigeans, 1691. [NAS.E69.11.1]
MILL, ALEXANDER, hearth tax, Arbirlot, 1691. [NAS.E69.11.1]
MILL, ALEXANDER, hearth tax, St Vigeans, 1691. [NAS.E69.11.1]
MILL, DAVID, hearth tax, St Vigeans, 1691. [NAS.E69.11.1]
MILL, DAVID, hearth tax, Arbirlot, 1691. [NAS.E69.11.1]
MILL, DAVID, hearth tax, St Vigeans, 1691. [NAS.E69.11.1]
MILL, HENRY, hearth tax, St Vigeans, 1691. [NAS.E69.11.1]
MILL, JAMES, tenant farmer in the Mains of Kellie, husband of Elspit Mill, born 1647, died 1672. [Arbirlot MI]
MILL, JAMES, hearth tax, Arbroath, 1691. [NAS.E69.11.1]
MILL, JOHN, hearth tax, Arbroath, 1691. [NAS.E69.11.1]
MILL, JOHN, hearth tax, St Vigeans, 1691. [NAS.E69.11.1]
MILL, JOHN, tenant of land in Punderlawfield, Arbroath, 1716. [NAS.E650/2]

MILL, PATRICK, hearth tax, St Vigeans, 1691.
[NAS.E69.11.1]
MILL, ROBERT, hearth tax, Arbirlot, 1691. [NAS.E69.11.1]
MILL, THOMAS, hearth tax, Arbirlot, 1691. [NAS.E69.11.1]
MILL, THOMAS, hearth tax, St Vigeans, 1691.
[NAS.E69.11.1]
MILL, WILLIAM, a merchant in Arbroath, 1794.
[NAS.CE70.1.8]
MILLER, DUNCAN, a weaver in Auchmithie, a Jacobite in 1745. [JA]
MILLER, GEORGE, a burgess of Arbroath, 1693. [ACB]
MILLER, JAMES, a mason in Fisheracre, St Vigeans, sasines, 1756, a deed, 1782, disposition of land there to his daughter Helen Miller in 1783. [NAS.CS238.M7.15; RS35.18.130, etc]
MILLER, JAMES, a baxter burgess of Arbroath, 1799. [AA. 18.941]
MILLER, JOHN, a baxter burgess of Arbroath, husband of Martha Horn, 1749. [Arbroath Abbey MI]
MILLER, THOMAS, a manufacturer burgess of Arbroath, 1794. [AA.18.941]
MILLER, WILLIAM, a merchant and auctioneer burgess of Arbroath, 1718. [AA.18.941]
MILLS, WILLIAM, a merchant in Arbroath, 1794.
[NAS.CE70.1.7]
MILNE, ALEXANDER, of Carriden, a burgess of Arbroath, 1684. [ACB]
MILNE, ALEXANDER, a burgess of Arbroath, 1685. [ACB]
MILNE, ALEXANDER, a currier burgess of Arbroath, 1797. [AA.18.941]
MILNE, CHARLES, a tailor burgess of Arbroath, 1791. [AA. 18.941]
MILNE, DAVID, a brewer burgess and guilds-brother, born 1738, died 1795, husband of Isabel Milne. [Arbroath Abbey MI]
MILNE, DAVID, a weaver burgess of Arbroath, 1797. [AA. 18.941]
MILNE, DUNCAN, a weaver burgess of Arbroath, 1799. [AA. 18.941]
MILNE, GEORGE, a farmer in Balcathie, Arbirlot, a Jacobite in 1745. [JA]
MILNE, JAMES, a burgess of Arbroath, 1681. [ACB]
MILNE, JAMES, a burgess of Arbroath, 1682. [ACB]

MILNE, JAMES, in Halton of Kinnell, a burgess of Arbroath, 1698. [ACB]

MILNE, JAMES, son of Alexander Milne, an apprentice glover in 1729, a master glover in 1738. [AER.95]

MILNE, JAMES, a merchant in Arbroath, sasine,1775. [NAS.RS35.25.231]

MILNE, JAMES, deacon of the baxters craft, born 1730, died 22 May 1778, husband of Elizabeth Horn; a deed, 1776. [Arbroath Abbey MI][NAS.CS27.1.19907]

MILNE, JAMES, a baker in Arbroath, husband of Margaret Dall, sasine,1779. [NAS.RS35.27.295]

MILNE, JAMES, a rope-maker burgess of Arbroath, 1793. [AA.18.941]

MILNE, JOHN, a burgess of Arbroath, 1681, a navigator in Arbroath, heir to Thomas Hamilton a bailie of Arbroath, 1686. [NAS.Retours.Forfar]

MILNE, JOHN, [1], hearth tax, Arbirlot, 1691. [NAS.E69.11.1]

MILNE, JOHN, [2], hearth tax, Arbirlot, 1691. [NAS.E69.11.1]

MILNE, JOHN, born 1713, tenant in Balcathy, died 1767, husband of Jean Smith, father of Elizabeth Milne, born 1743, died 1764. [Arbirlot MI]

MILNE, JOHN, convenor of the trades of Arbroath, formerly a wright in Barngreen, grandson of Thomas Thomson a burgess of Arbroath, sasine, 1747. [NAS.RS35.16.474]

MILNE, JOHN, a gardener in Arbroath, sasine, 1769. [NAS.RS35.22.447]

MILNE, JOHN, a wheel-wright burgess of Arbroath, 1797. [AA.18.941]

MILNE, MARION, born 1719, died 1770, wife of George Nicol a wright in Bonnyton. [Arbirlot MI]

MILNE, PATRICK, in Newton of Arbirlot, a burgess of Arbroath, 1685. [ACB]

MILNE, PATRICK, tenant of Ward Mill, a burgess of Arbroath, 1702. [ACB]

MILNE, PETER, a school-master burgess of Arbroath, 1791. [AA.18.941]

MILNE, ROBERT, in New Miln, a burgess of Arbroath, 1682. [ACB]

MILNE, ROBERT, in Millhill, a burgess of Arbroath, 1688. [ACB]

MILNE, WILLIAM, a burgess of Arbroath, 1683. [ACB]

MITCHELL, ALEXANDER, a mason in Arbroath, sasine, 1777. [NAS.RS35.26.493]

MITCHELL, ANDREW, in Arbroath, 1753. [NAS.E326.1.133]

MITCHELL, DAVID, a tanner in Arbroath, third son of Andrew Mitchell, a tenant farmer in Fife, and his wife Janet Reid, 1774. [NAS.SC20.36.12]

MITCHELL, JAMES, a shoe-maker burgess of Arbroath, 1799. [AA.18.941]

MITCHELL, JOHN, hearth tax, Arbirlot, 1691. [NAS.E69.11.1]

MITCHELL, JOHN, a merchant in Arbroath, 1718. [NAS.AC9.641]

MITCHELL, JOHN, a merchant in Arbroath, sasine, 1769. [NAS.RS35.22.392, etc]

MITCHELL, JOHN, master of the Cecilia of Arbroath, trading with Konigsberg in 1743, and of the Charming Peggy of Arbroath, 1770. [NAS.E504.24.1; E504.1.2; CE53.1.6]

MITCHELL, JOHN, a shoe-maker burgess of Arbroath, 1797. [AA.18.941]

MOIR, JOHN, a weaver burgess of Arbroath, 1797. [AA.18.941]

MOIR, ..., landowner of New Grange, 1770. [DLS.26]

MOLLESON, THOMAS, a burgess of Arbroath, 1800. [NAS.GD2.103]

MONCUR, WILLIAM, clerk of the shoe-makers craft of Arbroath, 1769. [AER.94]

MONTEATH, JAMES, of Alcart, a burgess of Arbroath, 1684. [ACB]

MONTGOMERY, MARGARET, spouse of James Philp of Almerieclose, a sasine, 1714. [NAS.RH8.1015]

MOODIE, DAVID, jr., a writer in Arbroath, 1744, 1753. [NAS.AC111.158B; E326.1.133]

MORE, ALEXANDER, born 1762, died at sea 1797. [Arbroath Abbey MI]

MORE, GEORGE, Provost of Aberdeen, a burgess of Arbroath, 1796. [AA.18.941]

MORES, GEORGE, a reed-maker in Kilbrachmont, a burgess of Arbroath, 1692. [ACB]

MORISDIE, JOHN, hearth tax, Arbroath, 1691. [NAS.E69.11.1]

MORISON, DUNCAN, Sergeant of the 3rd Regiment, a burgess of Arbroath, 1797. [AA.18.941]
MORISON, GEORGE, a manufacturer burgess of Arbroath, 1798. [AA.18.941]
MORIESON, JOHN, hearth tax, Arbroath, 1691. [NAS.E69.11.1]
MORISON, PATRICK, a shoe-maker in Arbroath, 1759. [AER.94]
MORRISON, ALEXANDER, a sawyer burgess of Arbroath, 1797. [AA.18.941]
MORTON, JAMES, hearth tax, Arbroath, 1691; a burgess of Arbroath, 1693. [ACB][NAS.E69.11.1]
MORTON, WILLIAM, a weaver burgess of Arbroath, 1797. [AA.18.941]
MOUR, ALEXANDER, a burgess of Arbroath, 1694. [ACB]
MUAT, JAMES, jr., a teacher in Edinburgh, by 1791 in Arbroath, divorce. [NAS.CS8.6.1068]
MUDIE, AGNES, relict of Thomas Fairweather, hearth tax, Arbroath, 1691. [NAS.E69.11.1]
MUDIE, ALEXANDER, a burgess of Arbroath, 1684; hearth tax, Arbroath, 1691. [ACB][NAS.E69.11.1]
MUDIE, ALEXANDER, a shoe-maker in Arbroath, 1765. [AER.94]
MUDIE, ANDREW, hearth tax, Arbroath, 1691. [NAS.E69.11.1]
MUDIE, DAVID, in Hilton, a burgess of Arbroath, 1681. [ACB]
MUDIE, DAVID, town clerk of Arbroath, 1760. [NAS.GD45.14.867]
MUDIE, DAVID, officer of the shoe-makers craft in Arbroath, 1760. [AER.94]
MUDIE, DAVID, a merchant in Arbroath, 1765. [NS.AD58.345]
MUDIE, HELEN, relict of Mr Alexander Auchterlonie, hearth tax, Arbroath, 1691. [NAS.E69.11.1]
MUDIE, JAMES, a wright burgess of Arbroath, a deed,1688. [NAS.RD2.69.520]
MUDIE, JAMES, in Gilchorn, a burgess of Arbroath, 1681; a councillor in 1681. [ACB][HHA.157]
MUDIE, JAMES, hearth tax, St Vigeans, 1691. [NAS.E69.11.1]

MUDIE, JAMES, in Arbroath, a Jacobite in 1745; a merchant burgess of Arbroath, testament, 1765, Comm. St Andrews. [NAS] [JA]
MUDIE, JAMES, born 1717, son of John Mudie and his wife Margaret Ogilvie in Auchmithie, a Jacobite in 1745. [JA]
MUDIE, JOHN, of Arbikie, a burgess of Arbroath, 1698. [ACB]
MUDIE, JOHN, of Gilchorn, a burgess of Arbroath, 1686, Justice of the Peace 1686, spouse of Christian Kinnear, hearth tax, 1691. [ACB][NAS.E69.11.1][RPCS.XI.574]
MUDIE, JOHN, a glover in Arbroath, 1736. [AER.95]
MUDIE, JOHN, stamp-master and a burgess of Arbroath, 1798. [AA.18.941]
MUDIE, PETER, a shoe-maker in Arbroath, 1738-1750. [AER.94]
MUDIE, ROBERT, a merchant in Arbroath, testament, 1742, Comm. St Andrews. [NAS]
MUDIE, WILLIAM, a merchant in Arbroath, brother of George Mudie a sailor, sasine,1763. [NAS.RS35.20.104, etc]
MUDIE, WILLIAM, late stamp-master in Arbroath, relict Margaret Mann, testament, 1776,Comm. St Andrews. [NAS]
MUDIE, WILLIAM, son of the late James Mudie, a merchant in Arbroath, testament, 1785, Comm. St Andrews. [NAS]
MUFFETT, AGNES, hearth tax, Arbroath, 1691. [NAS.E69.11.1]
MUIR, ALEXANDER, a skipper burgess of Arbroath, 1790. [AA.18.941]
MUIR, JAMES, born 1743, a skipper in Arbroath, died 1803, husband of Mary Dingwall, parents of James (1774-1806); testament, 1806, Comm. St Andrews. [NAS] [Arbroath Abbey MI]
MUNRO, HENRY, hearth tax, Arbroath, 1691. [NAS.E69.11.1]
MURESON, PATRICK, a shoe-maker burgess, husband of Nicola Guthrie, 1743. [Arbroath Abbey MI]
MURRAY, DAVID, hearth tax, St Vigeans, 1691. [NAS.E69.11.1]
MURRAY, JOHN, of Arthurstone, a burgess of Arbroath, 1684. [ACB]
MURRAY, Captain, a burgess of Arbroath, 1694. [ACB]

MCDONALD, JAMES, a weaver burgess of Arbroath, 1797. [AA.18.941]
MCDONALD, JOHN, a mason burgess of Arbroath, 1798. [AA.18.941]
NAIRN, CHARLES, a weaver burgess of Arbroath, 1797. [AA.18.941]
NAIRN, JAMES, a mariner in Arbroath, testament, 1787, Comm. St Andrews. [NAS]
NAIRN, JAMES, a weaver burgess of Arbroath, 1798. [AA.18.941]
NAIRN, JOHN, a burgess of Arbroath, 1693. [ACB]
NAIRN, PATRICK, son of Alexander Nairn, a seaman in Arbroath, testament, 1787, Comm. St Andrews. [NAS]
NAIRN, WILLIAM, a sailor in Arbroath, husband of Isobel Wilkie, 1753. [AER.82]
NAPIER, DAVID, a burgess of Arbroath, 1693. [ACB]
NAPIER, JAMES, in Arbroath, a Jacobite in 1745. [JA]
NAPIER, JOHN, born 1716, died 1764, a weaver burgess and freeman, husband of Elizabeth Horn. [Arbroath Abbey MI]
NAPIER, JOSEPH, a merchant burgess of Arbroath, 1792. [AA.18.941]
NEISH, ALEXANDER, tenant farmer in Boath, later residing in Arbroath, testament, 1774, Comm. St Andrews. [NAS]
NEISH, ALEXANDER, a manufacturer in Arbroath, sasine, 1780. [NAS.RS35.28.242]
NEISH, DUNCAN, schoolmaster at Arbirlot, 1690. [SHS.4.2]
NEISH, JOHN, a merchant in Arbroath, 1737, 1739. [NAS.AC9.1366, 1411]
NEISH, JOHN, a merchant in Arbroath, sasine, 1775. [NAS.RS35.25.325]
NEISH, PATRICK, a farmer in Arbroath, testament, 1791, Comm. St Andrews. [NAS]
NEISH, WILLIAM, a merchant in Arbroath, sasine, 1779. [NAS.RS35.27.392]
NEWTON, GEORGE, a merchant in Arbroath, testament, 1786, Comm. St Andrews. [NAS]
NICOLL, ALEXANDER, a militiaman Arbroath, 1685; a burgess of hearth tax, Arbroath, 1691. [ACB] [NAS.E69.11.1]
NICOLL, GEORGE, deacon of the tailors, husband of Euphan Hood, 1758. [Arbroath Abbey MI]
NICOL, JAMES, a tailor in Arbroath, a Jacobite in 1745. [JA]

NICOL, JOHN, a writer burgess of Arbroath, 1797. [AA. 18.941]
NICOL, ROBERT, a smith burgess of Arbroath, 1797. [AA. 18.941]
NICOLL, WILLIAM, a burgess of Arbroath, 1692. [ACB]
NICOLSON, ALEXANDER, hearth tax, Arbroath, 1691. [NAS.E69.11.1]
NIGHTMAN, THOMAS, a butcher burgess of Arbroath, 1795. [AA.18.941]
NISH, WILLIAM, hearth tax, Arbirlot, 1691. [NAS.E69.11.1]
NIVEN, JOHN, in Peebles, by Arbroath, a burgess of Arbroath, 1790. [AA.18.941]
NUCKOLL, ALEXANDER, hearth tax, Arbroath, 1691. [NAS.E69.11.1]
OGILVIE, DAVID, a burgess of Arbroath, 1683; hearth tax, Arbroath, 1691. [NAS.E69.11.1][ACB]
OGILVIE, DAVID, a merchant in Arbroath, spouse Isobel Fairweather, sasine,1730. [NAS.RS35.14.597]
OGILVIE, DAVID, master of the Isobell of Arbroath, 1739-1742, trading with Norway, Riga, and England; master of the Alexander and Jean of Arbroath, trading with Norway in 1743. [NAS.CE53.1.3; E54.24.1]
OGILVIE, JAMES, brother-german of Sir Francis Ogilvie of New Grange, late clerk to the Regality of Arbroath, testament, 1692, Comm. St Andrews. [NAS]
OGILVIE, JOHN, baillie of the Regality of Arbroath, 1706. [NAS.GD16.26.1.204]
OGILVIE, MARGARET, spouse of Alexander Robertson in Arbroath, 1684. [AA.A1.14.60]
OGILVIE, or BEATON, MARION, dead by 1657, mother of Mr Alexander Beaton, also dead by 1657. [RGS.X.605]
OGILVIE, THOMAS, governor of James, Lord Ogilvy, admitted as a burgess of Arbroath in 1710. [NAS.GD234.14.5.1]
OGILVIE, THOMAS, a merchant in Dundee, admitted as a burgess of Arbroath in 1729. [NAS.NRAS#0334]
OGILVIE, WILLIAM, a burgess of Arbroath, 1683. [ACB]
ORIM, HENRY, a burgess of Arbroath, 1688. [ACB]
ORKNEY, JOHN, a skipper in Arbroath, husband of Jean Grant, 1787. [NAS.S/H]
OSWALD, JAMES, of Phinkeltoun, a burgess of Arbroath, 1684. [ACB]

OUCHTERLONY, ALEXANDER, a glover in Arbroath, 1736. [AER.95]

OUCHTERLONY, ALEXANDER, a bailie of Arbroath, husband of Agnes Wallace, 1741. [Arbroath Abbey MI]

OUCHTERLONY, ALEXANDER, a writer in Arbroath, a Jacobite in 1745, 1758. [JA][NAS.E326.1.133]

OUCHTERLONY, GEORGE, late Provost of Arbroath, testament, 1731, Comm. St Andrews. [NAS]

OUCHTERLONY, JOHN, tenant of lands in Punderlawfield, Arbroath, 1716. [NAS.E650/2]

OUCHTERLONY, JOHN, born 1743, Provost of Arbroath, died 1804, husband of Isabella, born 1739, died 1818. [Arbroath Abbey MI]

OUCHTERLONIE, PATRICK, master of the Clementina of Arbroath trading with Rotterdam in 1726, of the Gloucester of Arbroath, 1739, and of the Goodwill of Arbroath, 1740, a smuggler, later a mariner in Maryland. [NAS.CE53.1.1/2/3; CS16.1.100]

OUCHTERLONY, ROBERT, of The Guynd, an Episcopal preacher in St Vigeans, a Jacobite in 1715. [HHA.170] [NAS.CH2.575.1]

PALMER, JOHN, born 1723, a workman in Arbroath, a Jacobite in 1745, later a soldier in Holland, died 1811. [HHA#174][JA]

PANTER, ELSPIT, hearth tax, Arbroath, 1691. [NAS.E69.11.1]

PANTON, JAMES, in Collairlie, a burgess of Arbroath, 1687. [ACB]

PATERSON, ALEXANDER, a weaver and freeman, born 1721, a weaver in Arbroath 1749, died 12 June 1761, husband of Helen Johnston. [Arbroath Abbey MI] [AER.93]

PATERSON, ANDREW, a brewer in Arbroath, 1768. [NAS.GD45.18.1983]

PATERSON, CHARLES, a flax-dresser burgess of Arbroath, 1798. [AA.18.941]

PATERSON, GEORGE, a skipper burgess of Arbroath, 1795. [AA.18.941]

PATERSON, JAMES, a baker and corn merchant in Arbroath, ledger, 1789-1798. [NAS.CS96.3223]

PATERSON, ROBERT, hearth tax, St Vigeans, 1691. [NAS.E69.11.1]

PATTERSON, ROSS, Sergeant of Captain Murray's Company of Colonel Row's Regiment, a burgess of Arbroath, 1699. [ACB]
PATERSON, ..., a wright burgess of Arbroath, 1797. [AA. 18.941]
PATON, JOHN, a wright burgess of Arbroath, 1689; hearth tax, Arbroath, 1691. [ACB][NAS.E69.11.1]
PATON, JOHN, servant to Mr George Maule, a burgess of Arbroath, 1693. [ACB]
PATON, WILLIAM, a weaver burgess of Arbroath, 1797. [AA.18.941]
PAUL, OLIVER, a burgess of Arbroath, testament, 1614, Comm. St Andrews. [NAS]
PAYMENT, ALEXANDER, hearth tax, Arbroath, 1691. [NAS.E69.11.1]
PEACOCK, DAVID, a weaver burgess of Arbroath, 1797. [AA.18.941]
PIERSON, A., a Notary Public and clerk of Arbroath, 1605. [HHA.143][ACB]
PEARSON, ADAM, a burgess of Arbroath, dead by 1649, father of James Pearson of Cairnie. [RGS.IX.2136]
PEARSON, Mr ALEXANDER, clerk of Arbroath, 1599. [LC.1378]
PEIRSON, ALEXANDER, in Ward Mill of Arbroath, 1609. [NAS.GD16.21.27]
PEIRSON, ALEXANDER, a burgess of Arbroath, 1630. [NAS.GD16.42.162]
PEIRSON, Mr ALEXANDER, of Balmadies, a burgess of Arbroath, 1683. [ACB]
PEARSON, ALEXANDER, of Smiddiecroft, a glover burgess of Arbroath, 1683, hearth tax, Arbroath, 1691, husband of Isabel Auchterlonie, sasines, 1686. [NAS.E69.11.1; RS35.S3.VIII.354; X.225]
PEARSON, ALEXANDER, a merchant in Arbroath, testament, 1687, Comm. St Andrews. [NAS]
PEARSON, ALEXANDER, master of the <u>Alexander and Jean of Arbroath</u>, 1740s, and the <u>Mary of Montrose</u>, a Jacobite in 1745, sasine,1770. [NAS.AC10/314; CE53.1.3/7; RS35.22.54] [JA]
PEARSON, Mr ARCHIBALD, at the Wardmill of Arbroath, 1599. [LC.1387]
PEARSON, Mr DAVID, of Cairnie, 1599. [LC.1378]

PEIRSON, DAVID, a burgess of Arbroath, 1607. [RGS.VI. 1990]
PEIRSON, DAVID, in Lochlands, a councillor of Arbroath, 1657, heir to his father David Pierson of Lochlands, Arbroath, 1667. [NAS.Retours.Forfar]
PEARSON, GEORGE, a burgess of Arbroath,1599, treasurer there,1606, sasine 1609, councillor 1617. [NAS.RS35.S1.1.141][HHA.143/150] [LC.1378] [RGS.VI.1497][RPCS.8.683]
PEARSON, GEORGE, in Arbroath, sasines, 1733. [NAS.RS35.15.302, etc]
PIERSON, HENRY, a burgess of Arbroath, husband of Jean Gray, sasine, 1642. [NAS.RS35.S2.II.511]
PIERSON, JAMES, of Cairnie, a burgess of Arbroath, 1601. [RGS.VI.1244]
PIERSON, Mr JAMES, son of Mr Alexander Pierson a writer in Arbroath, 1614; 1624. [RGS.VI.1071; VIII.841]
PEARSON, JAMES, clerk of Arbroath, sasine, 1717. [NAS.RS35.13.324]
PIERSON, JAMES, clerk of Arbroath, 1650, councillor in 1657. [HHA.156]
PIERSON, JAMES, heir to his father James Pierson burgh clerk of Arbroath, 1666. [NAS.Retours, Forfar]
PIERSON, JAMES, of Balmachie, a burgess of Arbroath, 1697. [ACB]
PEARSON, JOHN, a skipper of Arbroath, deeds, 1677,1680; master of the Dove of Montrose, trading with Norway, 1681, a burgess of Arbroath, 1686. [NAS.E72.16.4; RD4.46.607; AC7.4][ACB]
PIERSON, JOHN, a burgess of Arbroath, 1687. [ACB]
PIERSON, THOMAS, of Lochlands, burgess of Arbroath, 1595; bailie there, 1601, 1617. [NAS.Cal.Deeds.49.102; RS35.S2.II.510][HHA.137/149][RGS.VI.1191]
PIERSON, THOMAS, heir to father David Pierson minister at Kirkcaldy, in lands of Lochlands, Arbroath, 1682. [NAS.Retours.Forfar]
PEARSON, THOMAS, a burgess of Arbroath, sasines, 1711. [NAS.RS35.12.208, etc]
PEARSON, WILLIAM, hearth tax, Arbroath, 1691. [NAS.E69.11.1]
PEDDIE, DAVID, in Arbroath, 1664. [NAS.GD45.16.1225]
PEDDIE, JOHN, in Arbroath, testament, 1687, Comm. St Andrews. [NAS]

PEDDIE, JOHN, a glover in Arbroath, 1730s. [AER.95]
PEDDIE, JOHN, born in Arbroath in 1703, son of John Peddie and his wife Jean Smith, a merchant in Arbroath, 1739, a Jacobite in 1745, transported to Maryland. [NAS.AC8/590][JA][TNA.T1.328]
PERT, JAMES, sr., a lobster fisher in Arbroath, 1768. [NAS.CE53.1.6]
PERT, JAMES, jr., a lobster fisher in Arbroath, 1768. [NAS.CE53.1.6]
PERT, ROBERT, a lobster fisher in Arbroath, 1768. [NAS.CE53.1.6]
PERT, WILLIAM, a lobster fisher in Arbroath, 1768. [NAS.CE53.1.6]
PETER, ALEXANDER, a merchant burgess of Arbroath, spouse of Isabel Mudie, testament, 1608, Comm. Edinburgh; councillor of Arbroath, 1617, treasurer, died 1630. [Arbroath Abbey MI][HHA.150]
PETER, ALEXANDER, a merchant burgess of Arbroath, 1645. [NAS.GD205.21.8]
PETER, ALEXANDER, a tailor burgess of Arbroath, 1797. [AA.18.941]
PETER, JAMES, a burgess of Arbroath, 1610. [HHA.147]
PETER, JAMES, in Millgait, Arbroath, 1658. [RGS.X.640]
PETER, JOHN, a surgeon in London, heir to his father John Peter a merchant burgess of Arbroath, 1685. [NAS.Retours.Forfar]
PETER, JOHN, a tailor burgess of Arbroath, 1797. [AA.18.941]
PETER, PATRICK, a merchant burgess of Arbroath, dead by 1658. [RGS.X.640; XI.444]
PETER, WILLIAM, a tailor burgess of Arbroath, 1797. [AA.18.941]
PETRIE, AGNES, hearth tax, St Vigeans, 1691. [NAS.E69.11.1]
PETRIE, ALEXANDER, a burgess of Arbroath, 1797. [AA.18.941]
PETRIE, ALEXANDER, a weaver burgess of Arbroath, 1797. [AA.18.941]
PETRIE, ANDREW, hearth tax, St Vigeans, 1691. [NAS.E69.11.1]
PETRIE, DAVID, a burgess of Arbroath, 1688. [ACB]
PETRIE, HENRY, tenant of land in Punderlawfield, Arbroath, 1716. [NAS.E650/2]

PETRIE, HENRY, a burgess of Arbroath, husband of Margaret Jarron (1732-1799). [Arbroath Abbey MI]

PETRIE, JAMES, and his son, hearth tax, St Vigeans, 1691. [NAS.E69.11.1]

PETRIE, JAMES, a wright burgess of Arbroath, 1798. [AA. 18.941]

PETRIE, JOHN, a maltman burgess of Arbroath, testament, 1659, Comm. Brechin. [NAS]

PETRIE, JOHN, hearth tax, St Vigeans, 1691. [NAS.E69.11.1]

PETRIE, JOHN, a tanner burgess, husband of Helen Butchart [1723-1773], [Arbroath Abbey MI]

PETRIE, JOHN, a manufacturer burgess of Arbroath, 1799. [AA.18.941]

PETRIE, ROBERT, hearth tax, St Vigeans, 1691. [NAS.E69.11.1]

PETRIE, ROBERT, a weaver burgess of Arbroath, 1797. [AA.18.941]

PETRIE, WILLIAM, a carter burgess of Arbroath, 1799. [AA.18.941]

PHILIP, ALEXANDER, hearth tax, St Vigeans, 1691. [NAS.E69.11.1]

PHILIP, HENRY, of Almerieclose, born 1572, MA St Andrews in 1592, minister at Arbroath from 1601 until 1627, husband of Isabel Paterson, parents of James, Thomas, Marjory, and Isabel. [F.5.423][RGS.VIII.84]

PHILIP, JAMES, [1], hearth tax, Arbroath, 1691. [NAS.E69.11.1]

PHILIP, JAMES, [2], hearth tax, Arbroath, 1691. [NAS.E69.11.1]

PHILIP, JAMES, a weaver burgess, 1746. [Arbroath Abbey MI]

PHILIP, JOHN, a merchant in Arbroath, 1721. [NAS.AC9.759]

PHILIP, ... in Lochlands, Arbroath, 1658. [RGS.X.640]

PHILP, JAMES, of Almerieclose, son of James Philp and his wife Margaret Graham, Justice of the Peace in 1686, Standard Bearer to James Graham of Claverhouse at the Battle of Killiecrankie in 1689. [RPCS.XI.574][JA]

PHILP, JAMES, of Almerieclose, son of Henry Philp of Almerieclose and Isabel Paterson, a bailie burgess of Arbroath, died 1634, testament, 1636, Comm. St Andrews. [NAS.CS96.1.82/96][F.5.423]

PHILP, JAMES, in Arbroath, 1658, 1663. [RGS.X.640; XI. 444]

PHILP, JAMES, of Almerieclose, father of James and others, 1677, 1686. [NAS.AC7.4]

PHILP, JAMES, of Almerieclose, tenant of lands in Keptie and Dishland, Arbroath, sasine, deed,1716; spouse Margaret Graham; testament, 1732, Comm. St Andrews. [NAS.E650/2; RS35.13.261, etc; RD4.116.1123]

PHILP, JOHN, of Almerieclose, a Jacobite in 1715, escaped to the Netherlands, joined the Dutch West India Company, Governor of St Martins in the Dutch West Indies, 1728; brother of James Philp, a sasine 1733. [JA] [NAS.RS35.15.37]

PHILP, PATRICK, tenant of land in Keptie, Arbroath, 1716. [NAS.E650/2]

PHILP, PETER, a merchant burgess of Arbroath, 1691, spouse Jean Leslie, sasine,1706. [NAS.RS35.11.215] [ACB]

PICKEMAN, ROBERT, a glover in Arbroath, 1737. [AER. 95]

PIPER, ALEXANDER, of New Grange, a bond, 1711. [NAS.RH8.505]

PITCAIRN, Mr GEORGE, a burgess of Arbroath, 1685. [ACB]

PITHIE, ROBERT, a hay-dresser burgess of Arbroath, 1797. [AA.18.941]

PLORIE, DAVID, hearth tax, St Vigeans, 1691. [NAS.E69.11.1]

PORTER, JOHN, in Arbroath, testament, 1673, Comm. St Andrews. [NAS]

POWRIE, DAVID, hearth tax, Arbroath, 1691. [NAS.E69.11.1]

PRESTON, ROBERT, MA, minister at Arbirlot, 1731 until 1758. [F.5.421]

PRIOR, ALEXANDER, a carter burgess of Arbroath, 1791. [AA.18.941]

PROCTOR, JOHN, a sawyer burgess of Arbroath, 1797. [AA. 18.941]

PURDIE, JAMES, M.A., minister at Arbroath from 1735 until 1737. [F.5.424]

RAIT, ALEXANDER, a miller at the Wardmiln of Arbroath, sasine,1751. [NAS.RS35.17.132]

RAIT, ANDREW, burgess of Arbroath, 1688; hearth tax, Arbroath, 1691. [NAS.E69.11.1][ACB]

RAIT, FRANCIS, son of William Rait of Cononsyth, standard-bearer to Captain James Ruthven of the Scots Regiment in the Netherlands, a deed, 1680. [NAS.RD2.51.702]

RAIT, JOHN, a skipper in Arbroath, testament, 1722, Comm. St Andrews. [NAS]

RAITT, ROBERT, a glover in Arbroath, 1733. [AER.95]

RAIT, THOMAS, master of the Mary of Arbroath, 1745,1748, trading with Norway; master of the Friendship of Arbroath, 1752, husband of Isabel Jeffrey. [NAS.E504.24.1; E504.1.4][AJ#230/232]

RAIT, ..., of Cononsyth, Justice of the Peace in Arbroath, 1686. [RPCS.XI.574]

RAMSAY, ALEXANDER, a burgess of Arbroath, 1689, hearth tax, 1691 [ACB][NAS.E69.11.1

RAMSAY, ALEXANDER, a mariner in Arbroath, testament, 1743, Comm. St Andrews. [NAS]

RAMSAY, DAVID, a burgess of Arbroath, husband of Elizabeth Pierson, 1602, 1609, bailie of Arbroath, 1617. [HHA.149][RGS.VI.1325][RPCS.VIII.790]

RAMSAY, DAVID, master of the Christian of Arbroath, trading with Norway and Rotterdam, 1684. [NAS.E72.16.12/13]

RAMSAY, DAVID, hearth tax, Arbroath, 1691. [NAS.E69.11.1]

RAMSAY, DAVID, Provost of Arbroath, deed, 1715. [NAS.RD4.117.379]

RAMSAY, GEORGE, hearth tax, Arbroath, 1691. [NAS.E69.11.1]

RAMSAY, JAMES, of Parkconnan, Justice of the Peace in Arbroath, 1686. [RPCS.XI.574]

RAMSAY, JAMES, master of the Grizel of Arbroath, 1747. [NAS.E504.1.2]

RAMSAY, JAMES, a merchant in Arbroath, relict Margaret Kenny, sasine, 1772. [NAS.RS35.24.10]

RAMSAY, JOHN, a bailie of Arbroath, 1653, spouse Janet, daughter of Andrew Auchterlonie, a sasine. [NAS.RS35.S2.IV.174][HHA.156/157]

RAMSAY, JOHN, of Kirkton, hearth tax, St Vigeans, 1691. [NAS.E69.11.1]

RAMSAY, JOHN, sometime bailie of Arbroath, relict Christian Kinneres, testament, 1703, Comm. St Andrews.
RAMSAY, JOHN, a merchant in Arbroath, 1765. [NAS.AD58.345]
RAMSAY, JOHN, a manufacturer burgess of Arbroath, 1797. [AA.18.941]
RAMSAY, THOMAS, a burgess of Arbroath, 1599, testament, 1609, Comm. Edinburgh. [RGS.VI.930][HHA.138]
RAMSAY, WALTER, a burgess of Arbroath, 1687, hearth tax, 1691, deacon of the wrights of Arbroath, testament, 1731, Comm. St Andrews. [NAS.E69.11.1][ACB]
RAMSAY, WILLIAM, a merchant in Arbroath, 1749. [NAS.AC9.1661]
RAMSAY, WILLIAM, a weaver burgess of Arbroath, 1797. [AA.18.941]
RANNIE, JAMES, hearth tax, Arbroath, 1691. [NAS.E69.11.1]
RANNY, JOHN, the elder, a burgess of Arbroath, spouse Margaret Pilmure testament 1636, Comm. St Andrews. [NAS]
RANNIE, JOHN, hearth tax, Arbroath, 1691. [NAS.E69.11.1]
RANNIE, WILLIAM, hearth tax, Arbroath, 1691. [NAS.E69.11.1]
RANNIE, WILLIAM, hearth tax, Arbroath, 1691. [NAS.E69.11.1]
RANIE, ..., master of the Jean of Arbroath, 1752. [AJ.259]
RATTREY, Mr THOMAS, of Middle Gourdie, a burgess of Arbroath, 1699. [ACB]
RAY, THOMAS, graduated MA at St Andrews University in 1581, minister at St Vigeans from 1618 to 1622, burgess of Arbroath 1618, husband of Barbara Dempster, parents of Joseph, James, Thomas and Elisabeth. [F.5.449]
READ, JOHN, in Arbroath, 1664. [NAS.GD45.16.1225]
READ, Captain JOHN, of the Customs yacht Caroline, sasine of Cairntoun and Barbers Croft, Arbroath, 1763, landowner of Cairnie, 1770. [DLS][NAS.GD45.16.1300]
REBAIRN, PATRICK, hearth tax, Arbroath, 1691. [NAS.E69.11.1]
REID, ALEXANDER, a weaver in Arbroath, relict Margaret Smith, sasine,1752. [NAS.RS35.17.541]
REID, ALEXANDER, in Arbroath, relict Helen Gowans, sasine, 1766. [NAS.RS35.21.451]
REID, ANDREW, hearth tax, Arbirlot, 1691. [NAS.E69.11.1]

REID, ANDREW, hearth tax, St Vigeans, 1691.
[NAS.E69.11.1]
REID, HENRY, hearth tax, Arbroath, 1691. [NAS.E69.11.1]
REID, ISOBEL, hearth tax, Arbroath, 1691. [NAS.E69.11.1]
REID, JAMES, former bailie of Arbroath, 1677. [NAS.AC7.4]
REID, JAMES, a burgess of Arbroath, 1688. [ACB]
REID, JAMES, hearth tax, St Vigeans, 1691. [NAS.E69.11.1]
REID, JAMES, a sailor in Arbroath, husband of Margaret
    Gillespie, 1752. [AER.83]
REID, JOHN, the elder and the younger, hearth tax, St
    Vigeans, 1691. [NAS.E69.11.1]
REID, PATRICK, hearth tax, Arbirlot, 1691. [NAS.E69.11.1]
REID, PATRICK, a brewer in Arbroath, testament, 1724,
    Comm. St Andrews. [NAS]
REID, ROBERT, a burgess of Arbroath, 1683. [ACB]
REID, ROBERT, a candle-maker burgess of Arbroath, 1795.
    [AA.18.941]
REID, THOMAS, hearth tax, Arbroath, 1691. [NAS.E69.11.1]
REID, WILLIAM, hearth tax, St Vigeans, 1691.
    [NAS.E69.11.1]
REID, WILLIAM, hearth tax, Arbirlot, 1691. [NAS.E69.11.1]
REID, WILLIAM, a shoe-maker in Arbroath, 1737. [AER.94]
REITH, JOHN, hearth tax, Arbroath, 1691. [NAS.E69.11.1]
RENNIE, ALEXANDER, a timber-man in Arbroath, 1677.
    [NAS.AC7.4]
RENNIE, GEORGE, a timber-man in Arbroath, 1677.
    [NAS.AC7.4]
RENNIE, JAMES, a bailie of Arbroath, and a shoe-maker in
    Arbroath, 1737. [AER.94]
RENNIE, JOHN, born 1650, a cordiner, died 1630. [Arbroath
    Abbey MI]
RENNIE, JOHN, a cordiner burgess of Arbroath, sasine, 1640.
    [NAS.RS35.S2.II.489]
RENNY, JOHN, a merchant baillie, born 1677, died 3 January
    1752, husband of Nicola Fitchet. [Arbroath Abbey MI]
RENNY, JOHN, a merchant in Arbroath, sasine, 1779.
    [NAS.RS35.27.398]
RENNY, ROBERT, a merchant in Arbroath, testament, 1734,
    Comm. St Andrews. [NAS]
RENNEY, WILLIAM, born 1672, bailie of Arbroath, died
    1714, husband of Kathren Forsyth, parents of Margaret,
    Patrick, John, James and George. [Arbroath Abbey MI]

RENTS, HERCULES, from Arbroath, a citizen of Cracow, Poland, 1579. [SIP.53]
REYNOLD, ROBERT, M.A., minister at St Vigeans from 1650 to 1665. [F.5.449]
RICHARDSON, JAMES, hearth tax, Arbirlot, 1691. [NAS.E69.11.1]
RIDDOCH, WILLIAM, hearth tax, St Vigeans, 1691. [NAS.E69.11.1]
RYND, ALEXANDER, a councillor of Arbroath, 1617. [HHA.150]
RHIND, ALEXANDER, a weaver in Arbroath, 1767. [AER.93]
RIND, DANIEL, hearth tax, Arbroath, 1691. [NAS.E69.11.1]
RIND, DAVID, hearth tax, Arbroath, 1691. [NAS.E69.11.1]
RHIND, THOMAS, convenor of the crafts of Arbroath, 1680. [HHA.289]
RITCHIE, ALEXANDER, a thread-maker in Arbroath, a Jacobite in1745, transported to the colonies. [JA]
RITCHIE, ALEXANDER, a merchant burgess of Arbroath, 1781, 1795. [AA.18.941][NAS.CS96.2037]
RITCHIE, CRISTIAN, hearth tax, Arbroath, 1691. [NAS.E69.11.1]
RITCHIE, GEORGE, in Arbroath, 1664. [NAS.GD45.16.2125]
RITCHIE, GEORGE, in Arbroath, sasine,1704. [NAS.RS35.10.373]
RITCHIE, JAMES, a burgess of Arbroath, 1693. [ACB]
RITCHIE, JOHN, hearth tax, Arbroath, 1691. [NAS.E69.11.1]
RITCHIE, JOHN, master of the <u>Grizell of Arbroath</u>, trading with Norway,1740s, and of the <u>Farmer of Arbroath</u>, 1750, master of the brig <u>Fanner</u>, trading with Norway and Danzig, 1750,husband of Helen Scott, 1752. [NAS.E504.24.1/2][AER.86]
RITCHIE, PATRICK, a weaver in Arbroath, admitted as a burgess and freeman of Arbroath in 1760, a weaver in Arbroath, 1765. [AA.CX.99][AER.94]
RITCHIE, PATRICK, a manufacturer in Arbroath, admitted as a freeman and guilds-brother of Arbroath in1774. [AA.X.98]; born 27 January 1738, died 29 March 1805. [Arbroath Abbey MI]
RITCHIE, PATRICK, a weaver burgess of Arbroath, 1797. [AA.18.941]

RITCHIE, WILLIAM, hearth tax, St Vigeans, 1691. [NAS.E69.11.1]

RITCHIE, WILLIAM, son of George Ritchie, in Arbroath, sasine, 1720. [NAS.RS35.13.480]

ROB, DAVID, a skipper in Arbroath, died at sea in 1774, husband of Margaret Spink, parents of David Rob a skipper who died in 1805, testament, 1806, Comm. St Andrews. [NAS][Arbroath Abbey MI]

ROBERT, PETER, a baker burgess of Arbroath, 1795. [AA.18.941]

ROBERTSON, ALEXANDER, a sailor in Arbroath, spouse of Katherine Christie, 1749. [AER.67]

ROBERTSON, ANDREW, hearth tax, Arbroath, 1691. [NAS.E69.11.1]

ROBERTSON, DAVID, a burgess of Arbroath, 1687. [ACB]

ROBERTSON, DAVID, a weaver burgess of Arbroath, 1797. [AA.18.941]

ROBERTSON, JAMES, hearth tax, Arbroath, 1691. [NAS.E69.11.1]

ROBERTSON, JAMES, a weaver in Arbroath, 1742. [AER.94]

ROBERTSON, JOHN, hearth tax, Arbirlot, 1691. [NAS.E69.11.1]

ROBERTSON, JOHN, a hay-dresser burgess of Arbroath, 1797. [AA.18.941]

ROBERTSON, THOMAS, from Willinborough, Northants, a burgess of Arbroath, 1684; hearth tax, Arbroath, 1691. [NAS.E69.11.1][ACB]

ROBERTSON, THOMAS, hearth tax, St Vigeans, 1691. [NAS.E69.11.1]

ROBERTSON, WILLIAM, a merchant in Arbroath, 1758, relict Isobel Pirrie, testament, 1775, Comm. St Andrews. [NAS.E326.1.113]

ROBERTSON, WILLIAM, a sailor in Arbroath, 1776. [NAS.S/H]

ROBSON, DAVID, hearth tax, St Vigeans, 1691. [NAS.E69.11.1]

ROGE, ANDREW, hearth tax, St Vigeans, 1691. [NAS.E69.11.1]

ROLLAND, JOHN, in Bankhead of Arbirlot, a burgess of Arbroath, 1698. [ACB]

ROLLAND, JOHN, a merchant in Arbroath, husband of Agnes Farquharson, sasine, 1745; landowner of

Auchmithie, 1770. [NAS.AC9.1669; RS35.23.473] [DLS.26]

ROSS, DAVID, a weaver burgess of Arbroath, 1797. [AA. 18.941]

ROSS, PATRICK, an Episcopalian minister in Arbroath, a Jacobite in 1715. [JA]

ROSS, ROBERT, a weaver burgess of Arbroath, 1797. [AA. 18.941]

RUTHVEN, ANDREW, hearth tax, Arbroath, 1691. [NAS.E69.11.1]

RUTHVEN, ANNA, hearth tax, Arbroath, 1691. [NAS.E69.11.1]

RUTHVEN, JAMES, a Lieutenant in Lord Murray's Regiment, a burgess of Arbroath, 1694. [ACB]

RUXTON, JAMES, a weaver burgess of Arbroath, 1797. [AA. 18.941]

RUXTON, JOHN, a weaver burgess of Arbroath, 1797. [AA. 18.941]

RUXTON, ROBERT, a weaver burgess of Arbroath, 1798. [AA.18.941]

SALMOND, JAMES, a burgess of Arbroath, 1683. [ACB]

SALMOND, JAMES, a Corporal of Lord Carmichael's Troop of Dragoons, a burgess of Arbroath, 1695. [ACB]

SAMSON, JOHN, a councillor of Arbroath, 1657. [HHA]

SANDIMAN, JOHN, hearth tax, St Vigeans, 1691. [NAS.E69.11.1]

SANDS, ROBERT, a weaver in Arbroath, 1761. [AER.93]

SCOTT, ALEXANDER, a wright burgess of Arbroath, 1797. [AA.18.941]

SCOTT, ALEXANDER, an ale-seller burgess of Arbroath, 1797. [AA.18.941]; a brewer, born 1766, died 27 November 1813, husband of Helen Mill (1776-1842). [Arbroath Abbey MI]

SCOTT, CHARLES, a weaver burgess of Arbroath, 1797. [AA.18.941]

SCOTT, DAVID, a cooper burgess of Arbroath, husband of Janet Henderson testament, 1621, Comm. St Andrews. [NAS]

SCOTT, DAVID, hearth tax, St Vigeans, 1691. [NAS.E69.11.1]

SCOTT, DAVID, hearth tax, Arbirlot, 1691. [NAS.E69.11.1]

SCOTT, DAVID, a tailor in Arbroath, a Jacobite in 1745, transported to Maryland. [JA]

SCOTT, DAVID, a ploughman in Arbirlot, a Jacobite in 1745. [JA]
SCOTT, DAVID, a wright in Arbroath, deed, 1752. [NAS.RD3.211.288]
SCOTT, DAVID, of Dunninald, a burgess of Arbroath, 1789. [AA.18.941]
SCOTT, JAMES, a weaver burgess of Arbroath, 1798. [AA.18.941]
SCOTT, JOHN, master of the Friendship of Arbroath, 1740. [NAS.CE53]
SCOTT, JOHN, a tailor burgess, husband of Elizabeth Kay (1707-1771). [Arbroath Abbey MI]
SCOTT, THOMAS, a surgeon apothecary in Arbroath, testament, 1720, Comm. St Andrews. [NAS]
SCOTT, WILLIAM, hearth tax, St Vigeans, 1691. [NAS.E69.11.1]
SCOTT, WILLIAM, landowner of Barberscroft, 1770. [DLS.26]
SCOTT, WILLIAM, in Arbroath, testament, 1782, Comm. St Andrews. [NAS]
SCRYMGEOUR, DAVID, hearth tax, Arbroath, 1691. [NAS.E69.11.1]
SCRYMGEOUR, JOHN, born 1655, sometime in Balgathie, died 1720, his wife Euphan Anderson, born 1642, died 1728. [Arbirlot MI]
SCRYMGEOUR, JOHN, hearth tax, St Vigeans, 1691. [NAS.E69.11.1]
SCRYMGEOUR, JOHN, hearth tax, Arbroath, 1691. [NAS.E69.11.1]
SCRYMGEOUR, ROBERT, died 1674, his daughter Anna Scrymgeour, died 1723. [St Vigeans MI]
SEERIN, JAMES, hearth tax, St Vigeans, 1691. [NAS.E69.11.1]
SELLAR, JOHN, hearth tax, Arbirlot, 1691. [NAS.E69.11.1]
SHAKART, DAVID, a burgess of Arbroath, testament, 1614, Comm. St Andrews. [NAS]
SHAKART, WILLIAM, a mariner in Arbroath, testament, 1615, Comm. St Andrews. [NAS]
SHAND, JAMES, hearth tax, Arbroath, 1691. [NAS.E69.11.1]
SHAND, WILLIAM, a shoe-maker burgess of Arbroath, 1791. [AA.18.941]
SHANKS, DAVID, hearth tax, St Vigeans, 1691. [NAS.E69.11.1]

SHANKS, DAVID, a weaver in Arbroath, a Jacobite in 1745. [JA]

SHANKS, JOHN, a burgess of Arbroath, 1697. [ACB]

SHANKS, JOHN, a weaver in Arbroath, a Jacobite in 1745. [JA]

SHANKS, JOHN, deacon of the shoe-makers craft in Arbroath, 1737; a burgess and deacon convenor of the Trades, died in August 17.... aged 37, husband of Helen Scott. [Arbroath Abbey MI][AER.94]

SHANKS, THOMAS, a tenant in Arbroath, 1663. [RGS.XI.444]

SHANKS, THOMAS, an officer of the shoe-makers craft in Arbroath, 1751. [AER.94]

SHANKS, THOMAS, a weaver burgess of Arbroath, 1798. [AA.18.941]

SHARPY, Mr HENRY, in Arbroath, 1799. [NAS.GD45.18.2012]

SHEPHERD, DAVID, a burgess of Arbroath, 1690. [ACB]

SHEPHERD, JAMES, a burgess of Arbroath, 1686. [ACB]

SHEPHERD, JAMES, a seaman in Auchmithie, ca.1796. [St Vigeans MI]

SHEPHERD, JOHN, hearth tax, St Vigeans, 1691. [NAS.E69.11.1]

SIM, JOHN, a weaver burgess of Arbroath, 1797. [AA.18.941]

SIMMERS, JOHN, born 1701, died 1786. [Arbroath Abbey MI]

SIMPSON, ALEXANDER, a glover from Edinburgh, a burgess of Arbroath, 1687. [ACB]

SIMPSON, ALEXANDER, an officer of the shoemaker craft in Arbroath, 1757. [AER.94]

SIMPSON, GEORGE, a brewer in Arbroath, 1724. [NAS.GD3.14.2.1.44]

SIMPSON, GEORGE, a weaver in Arbroath, 1744. [AER.94]

SIMSON, JAMES, hearth tax, Arbirlot, 1691. [NAS.E69.11.1]

SIMPSON, JAMES, a shoe-maker in Arbroath, a Jacobite in 1745, transported to Maryland. [JA]

SIMPSON, JOHN, a brabiner burgess, husband of Janet Jack testament, 1600, Comm. St Andrews. [NAS]

SIMPSON, JOHN, a burgess of Arbroath, 1684, hearth tax, Arbroath, 1691. [NAS.E69.11.1][ACB]

SIMPSON, JOHN, a carter burgess of Arbroath, 1791. [AA.18.941]

SIMPSON, ..., master of a smack of Arbroath, wrecked off Carlingford, Ireland, in 1799. [AJ.2669]
SIMSON, ELSPET, hearth tax, Arbroath, 1691. [NAS.E69.11.1]
SINCLAIR, JOHN, burgh piper of Arbroath, a Jacobite in 1745. [JA]
SKINNER, ..., a burgess of Arbroath, 1678. [HHA]
SMALL, JOHN, a weaver burgess of Arbroath, 1798. [AA.18.941]
SMART, JAMES, hearth tax, St Vigeans, 1691. [NAS.E69.11.1]
SMART, ROBERT, the elder and the younger, hearth tax, St Vigeans, 1691. [NAS.E69.11.1]
SMITH, ALEXANDER, a barber in Arbroath, a Jacobite in 1745, transported to Maryland. [JA]
SMITH, ALEXANDER, born 1723, died 1779, husband of Margaret Speid. [St Vigeans MI]
SMITH, ALEXANDER, son of ..... Smith and Catherine Taup, who died 1754, a master mariner of the Royal Navy. [Arbroath Abbey MI]
SMITH, ANDREW, from Dundee, a burgess of Arbroath, 1699. [ACB]
SMITH, DAVID, hearth tax, Arbroath, 1691. [NAS.E69.11.1]
SMITH, ELIZABETH, hearth tax, Arbroath, 1691. [NAS.E69.11.1]
SMITH, JAMES, hearth tax, Arbirlot, 1691. [NAS.E69.11.1]
SMITH, JAMES, a burgess of Arbroath, 1687, hearth tax, 1691. [NAS.E69.11.1]
SMITH, JAMES, born 1698, a mariner who died in Antigua during 1745, husband of Isobel Lawson. [Arbroath Abbey MI]
SMITH, JAMES, of Strouckhill, also in Middelburg, Zealand, formerly in Arbroath, spouse Margaret Gavin, sasine, 1709. [NAS.RS35.12.9]
SMITH, JAMES, a mason burgess of Arbroath, died 16 June 1753, husband of Katherine Spink. [Arbroath Abbey MI]
SMITH, JAMES, a weaver in Arbroath, 1758. [AER.94]
SMITH. JAMES, a shoe-maker burgess of Arbroath, 1791. [AA.18.941]
SMITH, JOHN, hearth tax, St Vigeans, 1691. [NAS.E69.11.1]
SMITH, JOHN, hearth tax, St Vigeans, 1691. [NAS.E69.11.1]
SMITH, JOHN, servant to the Earl of Northesk, a burgess of Arbroath, 1693. [ACB]

SMITH, JOHN, master of the Margaret of Arbroath, 1743.
[NAS.E504.1.1]
SMITH, JOHN, a weaver burgess of Arbroath, 1797. [AA.
18.941]
SMITH, PATRICK, hearth tax, Arbirlot, 1691.
[NAS.E69.11.1]
SMITH, ROBERT, former miller at Ward Milne of Arbroath,
spouse Jean Ritchie, sasine, 1720. [NAS.RS35.13.480]
SMITH, ROBERT, a shoe-maker in Arbroath, 1740s. [AER.
94]
SMITH, ROBERT, a flax-dresser burgess of Arbroath, 1797.
[AA.18.941]
SMITH, THOMAS, a merchant burgess of Arbroath, 1797.
[AA.18.941]; died 4 February 1813 aged 70, husband of
Jean Gardner (1742-1796). [Arbroath Abbey MI]
SMITH, THOMAS, a flax-dresser burgess of Arbroath, 1798.
[AA.18.941]
SMITH, WILLIAM, hearth tax, St Vigeans, 1691.
[NAS.E69.11.1]
SMITH, WILLIAM, tenant of land in Punderlawfield,
Arbroath, 1716. [NAS.E650/2]
SMITH, WILLIAM, master of the Katherine of Arbroath,
1740s; husband of Mary Scott, 1753. [NAS.E504.24.1;
E504.1.2][AER.80][AJ.151/191/230]
SMITH, WILLIAM, a thread-maker in Arbroath, a Jacobite in
1745, transported to Maryland. [JA]
SMITH, WILLIAM, a blacksmith burgess of Arbroath, 1795.
[AA.18.941]
SMITH, ..., a burgess of Arbroath, 1683. [ACB]
SMITHSON, SAMUEL, in Lothbury, London, a burgess of
Arbroath, 1790. [AA.18.941]
SMYTH, JAMES, a weaver burgess of Arbroath, 1797. [AA.
18.941]
SOUTAR, DAVID, tenant of Ward Mill, Arbroath, 1650.
[HHA]
SOUTAR, JAMES, a merchant in Arbroath, a Jacobite in
1745. [JA]
SOUTAR, JOHN, a wright in Arbroath, 1778.
[NAS.RS35.27.94]
SOUTAR, JOHN, a cabinetmaker burgess of Arbroath, 1795.
[AA.18.941]
SOUTAR, JOHN, a merchant burgess of Arbroath, 1795. [AA.
18.941]

SOUTAR, ROBERT, in Tarry by Arbroath, 1724.
[NAS.GD3.14.2.1.44]

SPENCE, ANDREW, hearth tax, Arbroath, 1691.
[NAS.E69.11.1]

SPENCE, ANDREW, hearth tax, Arbroath, 1691; a burgess of Arbroath, 1693. [ACB][NAS.E69.11.1]

SPENCE, JAMES, a burgess of Arbroath, 1683. [ACB]

SPENCE, WILLIAM, [1], hearth tax, Arbirlot, 1691.
[NAS.E69.11.1]

SPENCE, WILLIAM, [2], hearth tax, Arbirlot, 1691.
[NAS.E69.11.1]

SPINK, ALEXANDER, a burgess of Arbroath, 1693. [ACB]

SPINK, ALEXANDER, hearth tax, St Vigeans, 1691.
[NAS.E69.11.1]

SPINK, ALEXANDER, master of the Mary of Arbroath, and later of the Lamb of Arbroath, trading with Norway in 1664-1673,.husband.of.Katherine.Kidd.
[NAS.RD4.56.783; E72.7.1/3; E72.16.1]

SPINK, ALEXANDER, a burgess of Arbroath, 1695. [ACB]

SPINK, ALEXANDER, a skipper in Arbroath, master of the Ninian of Arbroath, 1705, 1708, master of a 36 ton boat of Arbroath, 1725; master of the Elizabeth of Arbroath, 30..tons,.trading.with.Scandinavia.in.1740s.
[NAS.AC9.166,945; AC11.7; E504.24.1/2]

SPINK, ALEXANDER, a merchant in Arbroath, husband of Elizabeth Simpson, 1739. [NAS.AC8/590]

SPINK, DAVID, a skipper of Arbroath, in Aberdeen 1665.
[ASW.513]

SPINK, DAVID, a skipper and boxmaster of the Fraternity of Seamen of Arbroath, master of the Providence of Arbroath trading with Norway1680s; hearth tax, 1691,sasine,1703; relict Janet Webster, deed, 1715.
[NAS.RS33.10.478; RD4.117.555; E72.16.5-18; E69.11.1; AA.A1.14.67]

SPINK, DAVID, a merchant in Arbroath, a deed,1697, 1708.
[NAS.AC11.7; RD2.8012.140]

SPINK, DAVID, a skipper in Arbroath, in Bordeaux, France, 1725; testament, 1734, Comm. St Andrews. [NAS]
[SIL#244]

SPINK, DAVID, born 1774, a seaman in Auchmithie, died 1814. [St Vigean's MI]

SPINK, HENRY, a burgess of Arbroath, 1687; hearth tax, Arbroath, 1691. [NAS.E69.11.1][ACB]

SPINK, JAMES, sr., a skipper of Arbroath, 1677;1704;a burgess of Arbroath, 1687; master of the Margaret of Arbroath, trading with Norway, Holland and France, 1680s; hearth tax, Arbroath, 1691. [NAS.AC.7.4; E69.11.1;AC8/23; E72.16.7-18][ACB]

SPINK, JAMES, a burgess of Arbroath 1673; councillor of Arbroath, 1681. [ACB][HHA.157]

SPINK, JAMES, hearth tax, Arbroath, 1691. [NAS.E69.11.1]

SPINK, JAMES, born 1688, master of the Cecilia of Arbroath, trading with Scandinavia and the Baltic 1740s, later of the Two Sisters of Arbroath, trading with Rotterdam, 1757, a smuggler, died 1761, husband of Katherine Balfour, parents of John, Margaret, and Elizabeth. [NAS.CE53.1.5][Arbroath Abbey MI]

SPINK, JAMES, jr. a skipper of Arbroath, master of the Providence of Arbroath, 1704, 1716; master of the Grizel, trading with Norway 1740s, husband of Katherine.[NAS.AC8/23; AC9.567; E504.24.1; E504.1.2][AER.68]

SPINK, JAMES, a weaver in Arbroath, 1750. [AER.94]

SPINK, JAMES, a fisherman in Auchmithie, possibly a smuggler, 1768. [NAS.CE53.1.5]

SPINK, JAMES, in Arbroath, 1783. [NAS.CS271.46476]

SPINK, JAMES, born 1761, a skipper in Arbroath, drowned off Lerwick in 1803. [Arbroath Abbey MI]

SPINK, JAMES, born in Arbroath 1800, settled in Darien, Georgia, died in Savanna, Georgia, 1823. [Daily Georgian: 21 November 1823]

SPINK, JOHN, the younger, a burgess of Arbroath, 1606. [ACB][HHA.143]

SPINK, JOHN, a seaman in Arbroath, testament, 1636, St Andrews. [NAS]

SPINK, JOHN, in Arbroath, 1655. [NAS.AC2.1]

SPINK, JOHN, the younger, a burgess of Arbroath, 1686. [ACB]

SPINK, JOHN, hearth tax, St Vigeans, 1691. [NAS.E69.11.1]

SPINK, JOHN, a skipper in Arbroath, master of the Providence of Arbroath, 1708, 1716, 1719, 1721, master of a 18 ton boat of Arbroath, 1725; master of the Fortune of Arbroath, trading with Norway,1737-1745, the Concord of Arbroath, trading with Virginia, 1740, the Bell of Arbroath, 1751; the Elizabeth and Bill of Arbroath, 1751, trading with Riga, England, and

Virginia. [NAS.AC8/98; AC9.567, 759, 945, 1360; AC13.1.241; E504.24.1; E504.1.4; CE53.1.3/5/8]

SPINK, JOHN, a skipper in Arbroath, testament, 1803, Comm. St Andrews. [NAS]

SPINK, NINIAN, a skipper in Arbroath, hearth tax, Arbroath, 1691, a burgess of Arbroath, 1606; master of the Ninian of Arbroath, 1708. [NAS.AC11.7; E69.11.1][ACB]

SPINK, PATRICK, a skipper of Arbroath, master of the Providence of Arbroath, 1716; the Clementina of Arbroath, 60 tons, 1720, testament, 1724 , Comm. St Andrews. [NAS]

SPINK, PATRICK, master of the Marshall of Arbroath, 1730-1743, trading with Italy and Spain; the Sea Nymph of Arbroath, 1739, the Concord of Arbroath, 1740, died at sea on return voyage from Virginia, 1740. [NAS.E508; AC9.567; AC11.68; AC11.160; AC13.1.260; CE53.1.1; CE70.11.1; E504.24.1/2]

SPINK, RINGAN, a skipper of Arbroath, in Aberdeen, 1668. [ASW.554]

SPINK, ROBERT, master of the Venture of Auchmithie, 1745. [NAS.E504.24.1]

SPINK, WILLIAM, master of a 20 ton bark of Arbroath, 1725. [NAS.AC9.945]

SPINK, WILLIAM, a sailor in Arbroath, husband of Elizabeth Gardner, dead before 1753. [AER.82]

SPINK, WILLIAM, a skipper in Arbroath, husband of Elspet Petri, 1752. [AER.87]

SPINK, WILLIAM, a skipper in Arbroath, testament, 1770, Comm. St Andrews. [NAS]

SPINK, WILLIAM, a baker burgess of Arbroath, 1789. [AA. 18.941]

STARK, AMBROSE, a tide surveyor at Arbroath, testament, 1772, Comm. St Andrews. [NAS]

STARK, Captain ARTHUR, in Arbroath, 1753. [NAS.E326.1.133]

STEEL, JAMES, in Arbroath, a Jacobite in 1745. [JA]

STEENSON, JAMES, hearth tax, St Vigeans, 1691. [NAS.E69.11.1]

STEPHEN, ANDREW, hearth tax, Arbroath, 1691. [NAS.E69.11.1]

STEVEN, DAVID, deacon of the weavers in Arbroath, 1680; hearth tax, Arbroath, 1691. [NAS.E69.11.1][HHA.289]

STEPHEN, JAMES, hearth tax, St Vigeans, 1691.
[NAS.E69.11.1]
STEVEN, JAMES, a weaver in Arbroath, 1766. [AER.94]
STEVEN, JOHN, a weaver in Arbroath, 1744. [AER.94]
STEPHEN, JOHN, a slater in Arbroath, husband of Margaret Auchterlonie, sasine, 1759. [NAS.RS35.19.22, etc]
STEVEN, MARGARET, hearth tax, Arbroath, 1691. [NAS.E69.11.1]
STEPHEN, Provost PATRICK, a maltman burgess of Arbroath, 1674; a bailie there 1681, hearth tax, Arbroath, 1691; a merchant and Provost of Arbroath, 1691, testaments, 1707, 1708, Comm. St Andrews.
[AA,A1.14.92] [NAS.E69.11.1] [RPCS.XVI.77/705] [ACB][HHA.157]
STEPHEN, ROBERT, a slater in Arbroath, relict Mary Gowans, sasine,1767. [NAS.RS35.21.451]
STEVEN, WILLIAM, hearth tax, Arbroath, 1691.
[NAS.E69.11.1]
STEVENSON, JAMES, a burgess of Arbroath, husband of Helen Lindsay, testament, 1606, Comm. St Andrews.
[NAS]
STEPHENSON, JAMES, a burgess in 1686, bailie of Arbroath, 1691, hearth tax, Arbroath, 1691.
[NAS.E69.11.1][RPCS.XVI.705][ACB]
STEVENSON, JAMES, a haydresser burgess of Arbroath, 1797. [AA.18.941]
STEPHENSON, JOHN, hearth tax, St Vigeans, 1691.
[NAS.E69.11.1]
STEVENSON, THOMAS, MD, born 1761, died 1799, husband of Ann Adam, born 1761, died 1847. [Arbroath Abbey MI]
STEPHENSON, WILLIAM, hearth tax, Arbroath, 1691.
[NAS.E69.11.1]
STEVENSON, WILLIAM, a maltman burgess of Arbroath, died 1664, aged 64; his relict Isobel Ranken, testament, 1677, Comm. St Andrews. [NAS.GD45.16.1225]
[Arbroath Abbey MI]
STEVENSON, WILLIAM, a maltman burgess of Arbroath, relict Margaret Gardine testament, 1724. St Andrews.
STEVENSON, WILLIAM, a weaver in Arbroath, 1748.
[AER.94]
STEWART, GEORGE, a weaver burgess of Arbroath, 1797.
[AA.18.941]

STEWART, JAMES, a skinner burgess of Arbroath, 1791. [AA.18.941]
STEWART, JAMES, from Arbroath, of the Royal Navy, testament, 1807, St Andrews. [NAS]
STEWART, WILLIAM, in Ethie, a maltman burgess of Arbroath, 1687. [ACB]
STEWART, WILLIAM, a merchant from Edinburgh, a burgess of Arbroath, 1694. [ACB]
STILL, JAMES, a saddler burgess of Arbroath, 1797. [AA.18.941]
STILLAR, WILLIAM, a weaver burgess of Arbroath, 1797. [AA.18.941]
STIRLING, ALEXANDER, master of the Clementina of Arbroath, trading with Virginia in 1734. [NAS.CE70.2]
STIVAN, DAVID, a tailor burgess of Arbroath, 1683; hearth tax, Arbroath, 1691. [NAS.E69.11.1][ACB]
STIVAN, GEORGE, a weaver burgess of Arbroath, 1797. [AA.18.941]
STIVAN, JAMES, a soldier of Lord Carmichael's Troop of Dragoons, a burgess of Arbroath, 1695. [ACB]
STIVAN, JOHN, a shoemaker burgess of Arbroath, 1797. [AA.18.941]
STIVAN, ROBERT, a slater in Arbroath, relict Mary Gowans, sasine, 1767. [NAS.RS35.21.451]
STIVAN, WILLIAM, from Dundee, a burgess of Arbroath, 1699. [ACB]
STIVEN, WILLIAM, a slater burgess of Arbroath, husband of Jean Scott died 2 February 1736. [Arbroath Abbey MI]
STIVAN, WILLIAM, born 1775, a skipper in Arbroath, died at sea 1823, spouse Margaret Air. [Arbroath Abbey MI]
STORRIER, ROBERT, a weaver burgess of Arbroath, 1797. [AA.18.941]
STOUTAR, JAMES, a brewer in Arbroath, a Jacobite in 1745. [JA]
STRACHAN, ABRAHAM, a burgess of Arbroath, husband of Elizabeth Mader, a sasine, 1638. [NAS.RS35.S2.1.294]
STRACHAN, ALEXANDER, tenant of lands of Tarrie, Arbroath, 1716. [NAS.E650/2]
STRACHAN, ANDREW, a cordiner burgess of Arbroath, 1669.
STRACHAN, GEORGE, son of Patrick Strachan, minister at St Vigeans, 1696. [F.5.450]

STRACHAN, ISOBEL, a widow in Arbroath, testament, 1613. Comm. St Andrews. [NAS]

STRACHAN, JAMES, a maltman burgess of Arbroath, testament, 1615, Comm. St Andrews. [NAS]

STRACHAN, JOHN, in Arbroath, testament, 1687, Comm. St Andrews. [NAS]

STRACHAN, JOHN, master of the Prince of Wales of Arbroath, 1736, and of the Friendship of Arbroath, 1741, trading with Norway, Spain and Holland, husband of Agnes Adam. [NAS.CE53.1.2/3; S/H]

STRACHAN, JOHN, husband of Anne Ouchterlonie, parents of ...... Strachan, born 1741, died 1779. [Arbroath Abbey MI]

STRACHAN, JOHN, born 1762, a skipper in Arbroath, died 1830. [Arbroath Abbey MI]

STRACHAN, JOHN, a weaver burgess of Arbroath, 1797. [AA.18.941]

STRACHAN, JOSEPH, master of the Friendship of Arbroath, 1742. [NAS.CE53]

STRACHAN, Mr PATRICK, graduated M.A. from Marischal College, Aberdeen, in 1637, minister at St Vigeans from 1665 to 1693, husband of Helen Erskine, parents of George, Anna, David and Margaret; hearth tax, St Vigeans, 1691. [NAS.E69.11.1; GD45.13.208][F.5.449]

STRACHAN, THOMAS, hearth tax, Arbroath, 1691. [NAS.E69.11.1]

STRACHAN, THOMAS, master of the Thomas of Arbroath, 1740s, trading with Norway and Sweden, a smuggler, husband of Isobel Spink. [AER.80]. [NAS.AC8/642; E504.24.1; E504.1.1/2; CE53.1.4]

STRACHAN, WILLIAM, a burgess of Arbroath, sasine, 1638. [NAS.RS35.S2.V.50]

STRACHAN, WILLIAM, a sawyer burgess of Arbroath, 1797. [AA.18.941]

STRATON, Mr JOHN, a schoolmaster from Alyth, a burgess of Arbroath, 1685; hearth tax, Arbroath, 1691; possibly an Episcopal preacher and a Jacobite in Arbirlot, 1715. [NAS.E69.11.1][ACB][JA]

STRATTON, JOHN, a burgess of Arbroath, 1689. [ACB]

STROAK, ANDREW, a weaver in Arbroath, 1758. [AER.94]

STROAK, DAVID, a weaver in Arbroath, 1746. [AER.9;3]

STORIE, GEORGE, hearth tax, St Vigeans, 1691. [NAS.E69.11.1]

STREIBER, AUGUSTUS, a burgess of Arbroath, 1790. [AA. 18.941]
STURROCK, ALEXANDER, a weaver burgess of Arbroath, 1797. [AA.18.941]
STURROCK, JAMES, hearth tax, Arbirlot, 1691. [NAS.E69.11.1]
STURROCK, JAMES, born 1707, died 1765, husband of Isabel Mudie, parents of James Sturrock a merchant in Tobago. [Arbirlot MI]
STURROCK, JAMES, a farmer in Arbroath, a Jacobite in 1745. [JA]
STURROCK, JAMES, a merchant in Arbroath, sasine, 1776; letters, 1779. [NAS.RS35.25.481; GD45.12.441; GD45.14.452]
STURROCK, JOHN, a weaver in Arbroath, sasine, 1775. [NAS.RS35.25.102]
STURROCK, JOHN, son of a weaver, a burgess of Arbroath, 1797. [AA.18.941]
STURROCK, PETER, a merchant burgess of Arbroath, 1797. [AA.18.941]
SUMMER, JAMES, hearth tax, St Vigeans, 1691. [NAS.E69.11.1]
SUTOR, JOHN, hearth tax, St Vigeans, 1691. [NAS.E69.11.1]
SUTTIE, JAMES, hearth tax, St Vigeans, 1691. [NAS.E69.11.1]
TAES, MALCOLM, hearth tax, Arbroath, 1691. [NAS.E69.11.1]
TAITT, WILLIAM, a carpenter from Leith, a burgess of Arbroath, 1685. [ACB]
TALBERT, JOHN, hearth tax, St Vigeans, 1691. [NAS.E69.11.1]
TAURE, ANDREW, hearth tax, Arbirlot, 1691. [NAS.E69.11.1]
TAVENDALE, ALEXANDER, a weaver burgess of Arbroath, 1795. [AA.18.941]
TAYLOR, DAVID, hearth tax, St Vigeans, 1691. [NAS.E69.11.1]
TAYLOR, DAVID, born 1731, brewer at Barngreen, Arbroath, died 1776, husband of Helen Smith. [Arbroath Abbey MI]
TAYLOR, JAMES, hearth tax, St Vigeans, 1691. [NAS.E69.11.1]

TAYLOR, JAMES, hearth tax, Arbirlot, 1691. [NAS.E69.11.1]
TAYLOR, ROBERT, in Arbroath, testament, 1676, Comm. St Andrews. [NAS]
TAYLOR, ROBERT, master of the Isobell of Auchmithie, 1744. [NAS.E504.24.1]
TAYLOR, ..., master of the Jean of Arbroath, 1752. [AJ#231]
TAYLOR, WILLIAM, a shoemaker burgess of Arbroath, 1792. [AA.18.941]
TELFORT, JOHN, jr., a sailor in Arbroath, 1752. [AER.69]
TEVIOTDALE, ALEXANDER, a weaver burgess, husband of Ann Williamson, 1796. [Arbroath Abbey MI]
THOM, JAMES, a sawyer burgess of Arbroath, 1797. [AA.18.941]
THOMSON, ALEXANDER, a shoemaker in Arbroath, 1750. [AER.94]
THOMSON, ANDREW, hearth tax, Arbirlot, 1691. [NAS.E69.11.1]
THOMSON, CHARLES, town clerk, a burgess of Arbroath, 1792. [AA.18.941]
THOMSON, Mr DAVID, a burgess of Arbroath, 1693. [ACB]
THOMSON, DAVID, a weaver in Arbroath, 1737. [AER.93]
THOMSON, JAMES, a weaver burgess of Arbroath, spouse Catherine Low testament, 1616, Comm. St Andrews. [NAS]
THOMSON, JAMES, in Kinnell, a burgess of Arbroath, 1693. [NAS]
THOMSON, JAMES, in Aberdeen, a burgess of Arbroath, 1791. [AA.18.941]
THOMSON, JAMES, a weaver burgess of Arbroath, 1797. [AA.18.941]
THOMSON, JOHN, a burgess of Arbroath, 1687; hearth tax, Arbroath, 1691. [NAS.E69.11.1][ACB]
THOMSON, Reverend ROBERT, born 1760, died 1826, husband of Alison Louson, born 1766, died 1808. [Arbroath Abbey MI]
THOMSON, THOMAS, a burgess of Arbroath, sasine,1745. [NAS.RS35.16.474]
THORN, JOHN, master of the Katherine of Easthaven 1747. [NAS.CE53.1.3]
TOD, WILLIAM, a burgess of Arbroath, 1685. [ACB]
TOSH, JOHN, a burgess of Arbroath, 1689. [ACB]

TOWARD, JOHN, hearth tax, Arbroath, 1691.
[NAS.E69.11.1]
TRAIL, JOHN, a wright burgess of Arbroath, 1795. [AA.
18.941]
TWADELL, JOHN, a shoemaker in Arbroath, 1743. [AER.94]
TWADDELL, ..., in Arbroath, 1658. [RGS.X.640]
VALENTINE, GEORGE, hearth tax, St Vigeans, 1691.
[NAS.E69.11.1]
VALENTINE, JAMES, hearth tax, Arbroath, 1691.
[NAS.E69.11.1]
VANNET, JAMES, a weaver in Arbroath, 1750, deacon of the
craft, 1749. [AER.94]
VANNETT, JOHN, a brewer, hearth tax, Arbroath, 1691.
[NAS.E69.11.1]
VANNETT, PATRICK, a burgess of Arbroath, 1695. [NAS]
VANNETT, PATRICK, treasurer of Arbroath, 1724.
[NAS.GD3.14.2.1.44]
VANNET, PATRICK, an officer of the shoemakers craft in
Arbroath, 1759. [AER.94]
VORE, JOHN, Adjutant of Lord Carmichael's Troop of
Dragoons, a burgess of Arbroath, 1695. [ACB]
WAELLS, GERET, a Lieutenant of Captain Murray's
Company in Colonel Row's Regiment, a burgess of
Arbroath, 1699. [ACB]
WALKER, HELEN, in Berryfauld, Arbroath, 1752. [AER]
WALKER, JAMES, a weaver burgess of Arbroath, 1797.
[AA.18.941]
WALKER, ROBERT, a saddler burgess of Arbroath, 1797.
[AA.18.941]
WALKER, WILLIAM, in Hercules Den, Arbroath, 1752.
[AER]
WALKER, WILLIAM, a smith in Arbroath, spouse Isobel
Sturrock, sasine, 1775. [NAS.RS35.25.253]
WALLACE, ANDREW, convenor of the trades of Arbroath,
1674.
WALLACE, DAVID, a maltman burgess of Arbroath,
testament, 1675, Comm. St Andrews. [NAS]
WALLACE, DAVID, son of John Wallace, a burgess of
Arbroath, 1696. [ACB]
WALLACE, DAVID, a merchant in Arbroath, deed,1715,
testament, 1721, Comm. St Andrews.
[NAS.RD4.117.640]

WALLACE, DAVID, a merchant and former bailie of Arbroath, 1753, petition, 1752; sasine, 1761. [NAS.E326.1.133; RS35.19.302; e785.5]

WALLACE, DAVID, master of the <u>Marischal of Arbroath</u> 1740, the <u>Robert and Mark of Arbroath,</u> 1749, the <u>Hopewell of Arbroath</u>, trading with Riga, Sweden, Holland and Portugal, husband of Marjory Watson; testament, 1758,Comm. St Andrews. [NAS] [NAS.CE53.1.3; E504.24.2][AER.87]

WALLACE, GEORGE, a mariner in Arbroath, sasine, 1733. [NAS.RS34.15.300]

WALLACE, J., a councillor of Arbroath, 1657. [HHA]

WALLACE, JAMES, a mariner in Elie, a burgess of Arbroath, 1683. [ACB]

WALLACE, JAMES, a merchant in Arbroath, 1733, 1737. [NAS.AC11/68; AC8/549]

WALLACE, JAMES, a sailor in Arbroath, 1767. [NAS.CE53.1.6]

WALLACE, JOHN, in Arbroath, 1627. [RPCS.II.23]

WALLACE, JOHN, [1] councillor and deacon of the shoemakers in Arbroath, 1681; hearth tax, Arbroath, 1691. [NAS.E69.11.1][HHA.157]

WALLACE, JOHN, [2], hearth tax, Arbroath, 1691. [NAS.E69.11.1]

WALLACE, JOHN, son of John Wallace, a burgess of Arbroath, 1696. [ACB]

WALLACE, JOHN, tenant of lands in Dishland and Keptie, Arbroath, 1716. [NAS.E650/2]

WALLACE, JOHN, a merchant in Arbroath, 1715, testament, 1723, Comm. St Andrews. [NAS.RD2.104.860]

WALLACE, JOHN, a merchant in Arbroath, testament, 1734, Comm. St Andrews. [NAS]

WALLACE, JOHN, master of the <u>Marischal of Arbroath</u>, and the <u>St Thomas of Arbroath</u>, trading with Maryland and Norway, 1740s, possibly a smuggler; testament, 1749, Comm. St Andrews. [NAS.CE53.1.3] [NAS.AC9.1500; E504.24.1; CE53.1.3]

WALLACE, JOHN, a merchant and Provost of Arbroath, sasines,1742, 1745, 1753. [NAS.RS35.16.134, etc; AC11.166; E326.1.133]

WALLACE, PATRICK, a councillor of Arbroath, 1657, husband of Isabel Granger, a sasine, 1657; Provost 1674-1681, father of John Wallace and Patrick Wallace,

1684, 1691. [HHA.156/157][NAS.RS35.S3.VIII.159; E69.11.1][AA.A1.14.107]

WALLACE, PATRICK, son of John Wallace, a burgess of Arbroath 1696; hearth tax, Arbroath, 1691; husband of (1) Helen Ouchterlony, a sasine, 1699; a merchant in Arbroath, deed, 1708; sasine, 1715; deed 1725; merchant and ex-provost of Arbroath, a Jacobite in 1745; spouse (2) Isobel Grainger, 1704.[JA] [NAS.RD2.104.860; RS35.S3.10.182/362; AC8/102; AC11.166; E60.11.1; GD3.14.2.1.54]

WALLACE, PATRICK, tenant of land in Punderlawfield, Arbroath, 1716. [NAS.E650/2]

WALLACE, PATRICK, a merchant in Arbroath, testament, 1734, Comm. St Andrews. [NAS]

WALLACE, PATRICK, a linen manufacturer and bailie of Arbroath, son of Provost Wallace, a Jacobite in 1745. [JA]

WALLACE, PATRICK, sr., Provost of Arbroath, 1717, testament, 1719, Comm. St Andrews. [NAS.E657.135]

WALLACE, PATRICK, a merchant in Arbroath, testament, 1754, Comm. St Andrews. [NAS.E326.1.133]

WALLACE, THOMAS, a merchant in Arbroath, 1722, sasine, 1743; testament, 1735, Comm. St Andrews. [NAS.AC9.839, 1500; RS35.14.328]

WALLACE, WILLIAM, a cordiner in Arbroath, father of Isabel Wallace, a sasine, 1666. [NAS.RS35.S3.III.380]

WALLACE, WILLIAM, hearth tax, Arbroath, 1691. [NAS.E69.11.1]

WALLACE, WILLIAM, son of John Wallace, a burgess of Arbroath, 1696; a merchant in Arbroath, and his wife Margaret Rait, sasine,1705. [NAS.RS35.11.320][ACB]

WALLACE, WILLIAM, late bailie in Arbroath, testament, 1734, Comm. St Andrews. [NAS]

WALLACE, WILLIAM, an ale-seller, a burgess of Arbroath, 1797. [AA.18.941]

WALLINTEIN, ALEXANDER, a burgess of Arbroath, 1682. [ACB]

WALLS, MARGARET, hearth tax, Arbroath, 1691. [NAS.E69.11.1]

WANNANT, JOHN, a burgess of Arbroath, 1689. [ACB]

WATSON, ANDREW, hearth tax, Arbroath, 1691. [NAS.E69.11.1]

WATSON, DAVID, a weaver in Arbroath, 1674, deacon of the weavers 1681. [HHA.157/289]
WATSON, GEORGE, a burgess of Arbroath, 1682. [ACB]
WATSON, JAMES, a burgess of Arbroath, 1697. [ACB]
WATSON, JAMES, a burgess of Arbroath, 1789. [AA.18.941]
WATSON, JOHN, a merchant and brewer burgess of Arbroath, husband of Annie Cargill, 16... [Arbroath Abbey MI]
WATSON, JOHN, a brewer in Arbroath, a Jacobite in 1745, transported to the colonies. [JA]
WATSON, JOSEPH, a skipper burgess of Arbroath, 1796. [AA.18.941]
WATSON, LILLIAS, daughter of the late John Watson of Thirty Acres, parish of Arbroath, testament, 1797, Comm. St Andrews. [NAS]
WATSON, RICHARD, educated at St Andrews, minister at Arbirlot from 1790 until 1829, husband of Isabel Balfour, parents of Elizabeth, and Richard. [F.5.421]
WATSON, THOMAS, hearth tax, St Vigeans, 1691. [NAS.E69.11.1]
WATSON, THOMAS, graduated M.A. from St Andrews in 1689, burgess of Arbroath, 1697; minister at St Vigeans from 1702 until 1725, testament, 1743, Comm. St Andrews. [NAS][F.5.450][ACB]
WATSON, THOMAS, a merchant in Arbroath, husband of Mary Scott 1742; a tobacconist in 1745, a Jacobite transported to the colonies. [NAS.AC9.1479][JA]
WATSON, WILLIAM, a skipper of Arbroath, 1704. [NAS.AC8/23]
WATSON, WILLIAM, a carter burgess of Arbroath, 1792. [AA.18.941]
WATSON, WILLIAM, a divinity student, a burgess of Arbroath, 1790. [AA.18.941]
WATT, GEORGE, a weaver burgess of Arbroath, 1797. [AA.18.941]
WATT, ROBERT, a brewer burgess of Arbroath, 1792. [AA.18.941]
WATT, WILLIAM, a weaver burgess of Arbroath, 1799. [AA.18.941]
WEAR, PATRICK, a weaver burgess, husband of Isabel Shepherd (1675-1711). [Arbroath Abbey MI]

WEBSTER, ALEXANDER, born 1646, tenant in Connon Mill, died 1723, wife Jean Shanks, born 1664, died 1714. [Arbirlot MI]

WEBSTER, ALEXANDER, a merchant in Arbroath 1677, councillor 1681, hearth tax, Arbroath, 1691; appointed by the Privy Council to collect funds to repair the pier in 1691. [NAS.E69.11.1; AC7.5][RPCS.XVI.77/705]

WEBSTER, ALEXANDER, a manufacturer burgess of Arbroath, 1797. [AA.18.941]

WEBSTER, ANDREW, a wright in Arbroath, a Jacobite in 1745. [JA]

WEBSTER, DAVID, a joiner in Arbroath, a Jacobite in 1745. [JA]

WEBSTER, DAVID, a brewer in Arbroath, a Jacobite in 1745. [JA]

WEBSTER, DAVID, a merchant in Arbroath, sasine, 1778. [NAS.RS35.26.493]

WEBSTER, FRANCIS, a merchant burgess of Arbroath, 1792. [AA.18.941]

WEBSTER, GEORGE, in Arbroath, testament, 1773, Comm. St Andrews. [NAS]

WEBSTER, JAMES, a labourer in Arbroath, testament, 1800, Comm. St Andrews. [NAS]

WEBSTER, JOHN, a merchant in Arbroath, 1677/1687, councillor 1681, hearth tax, Arbroath, 1691. [NAS.E69.11.1; AC7.4/8][HHA.157]

WEBSTER, JOHN, a sailor in Arbroath, a Jacobite in 1745. [JA]

WEBSTER, JOHN, from St Vigeans, a Jacobite in 1745. [JA]

WEBSTER, JOHN, landowner of Smiddycroft, 1770. [DLS. 26]

WEBSTER, ROBERT, a weaver in Arbroath, 1763. [AER.93]

WEEMS, JOHN, Ensign of Captain Murray's Company in Colonel Row's Regiment, a burgess of Arbroath, 1699. [ACB]

WELSH, ANN, a schoolmistress in Arbroath, 1788. [NAS.B59.24.6.91]

WELSH, JAMES, in Kingston, Jamaica, a burgess of Arbroath, 1789. [AA.18.941]

WESTERN, WALLACE, Lieutenant of the 134th Regiment, a burgess of Arbroath, 1795. [AA.18.941]

WHITE, JANET, hearth tax, Arbroath, 1691. [NAS.E69.11.1]

WHITLAW, ALEXANDER, hearth tax, St Vigeans, 1691.
[NAS.E69.11.1]
WHITLAW, JAMES, hearth tax, St Vigeans, 1691.
[NAS.E69.11.1]
WHYTE, DAVID, deacon of the glovers craft in Arbroath, 1737. [AER.95]
WICHTAN, ANDREW, a maltman burgess of Arbroath, testament, 1636, Comm. St Andrews. [NAS]
WICHTAN, DAVID, a maltman burgess of Arbroath, husband of Margaret Lauder testament, 1617, Comm. St Andrews. [NAS]
WICHTAN, DAVID, a burgess of Arbroath, husband of Janet Hunter, a sasine, 1620. [NAS.RS35.S1.I.162]
WILKIE, JOHN, son of Thomas Wilkie and Margaret Spink, a skipper in Arbroath, 1779. [NAS.S/H][AER.67]
WILKIE, ROBERT, born 1725, a merchant skipper in Arbroath, died 1799, husband of Christian Petrie, sasine. [NAS.RS34.22.178; S/H][Arbroath Abbey MI]
WILKIE, THOMAS, born 1729, son of Thomas Wilkie and Magdalene Spink, master of the John and David of Arbroath, trading with Portugal and Scandinavia in the 1740s, a smuggler, a Jacobite in1745. [NAS.E504.24.1; CE53.1.3] [JA]
WILKIE, WILLIAM, a weaver in Arbroath, sasine,1776. [NAS.RS35.25.449]
WILL, JAMES, deacon of the bakers of Arbroath, 1681. [HHA.157]
WILLIAMSON, ALEXANDER, hearth tax, Arbroath, 1691. [NAS.E69.11.1]
WILLIAMSON, ANDREW, hearth tax, Arbirlot, 1691. [NAS.E69.11.1]
WILLIAMSON, DAVID, a burgess of Arbroath, 1689; hearth tax, Arbroath, 1691. [NAS.E69.11.1] [ACB]
WILLIAMSON, JAMES, hearth tax, Arbroath, 1691. [NAS.E69.11.1]
WILLIAMSON, JOHN, jr., a weaver burgess of Arbroath, 1795. [AA.18.941]
WILLIAMSON, ROBERT, from Arbroath, a citizen of Bergen, Norway, 16... [SAB]
WILLIAMSON, WILLIAM, hearth tax, Arbroath, 1691. [NAS.E69.11.1]
WILLIAMSON, WILLIAM, a merchant in Arbroath, testament, 1750, Comm. St Andrews. [NAS]

WILSON, DAVID, a brewer in Arbroath, a Jacobite in 1745. [JA]
WILSON, DAVID, a weaver burgess of Arbroath, 1797. [AA. 18.941]
WILSON, JAMES, a skipper in Arbroath, 1701. [NAS.RD4.88.33]
WILSON, JAMES, a weaver in Arbroath, 1739. [AER.93]
WILSON, JOHN, son of Thomas Wilson in Tarrie, St Vigeans, a Jacobite in 1745. [JA]
WILSON, JOHN, master of the John of Arbroath, trading with Norway, 1686. [NAS.E72.16.18]
WILSON, JOHN, hearth tax, Arbirlot, 1691. [NAS.E69.11.1]
WILSON, JOHN, a mariner of Arbroath, 1705. [NAS.AC9.166]
WILSON, JOHN, a weaver in Arbroath, testament, 1735, Comm. St Andrews. [NAS]
WILSON, JOHN, master of the Agnes of Arbroath, a brig, 1741. [NAS.AC8/610]
WINDRUM, ALEXANDER, a merchant in Arbroath, 1730s. [AER.95]
WINDRUM, JAMES, a burgess of Arbroath, 1688. [ACB]
WINDRUM, JAMES, a weaver burgess of Arbroath, 1797. [AA.18.941]
WISHART, MARGARET, hearth tax, Arbroath, 1691. [NAS.E69.11.1]
WISHART, WILLIAM, a merchant in Arbroath, spouse Elspeth Fithie, sasine, 1704. [NAS.RS35.10.362, etc]
WOOD, ANDREW, in Lochlands, Arbroath, 1658. [RGS.X.640]
WOOD, DAVID, a merchant in Arbroath, sasine, 1704. [NAS.RS35.10.340]
WOOD, JAMES, a burgess of Arbroath, husband of Isabel Hunter, a councillor 1617, sasine 1620. [NAS.RS35.S1.1.162][HHA.150]
WOOD, JAMES, a tenant in Arbroath, 1653, 1663, a burgess of Arbroath, 1669. [RGS.X.640, XI.444] [NAS.RS35.S3.IV.260]
WOOD, Sir JAMES, of Bonnitoun, hearth tax, St Vigeans, 1691. [NAS.E69.11.1]
WOOD, JAMES, in Arbroath, sasines,1733. [NAS.RS35.15.37, etc]
WOOD, Mr JOHN, son of Sir John Wood of Bonnyton, a burgess of Arbroath, 1692. [ACB]
WOOD, ..., of Allardie, St Vigeans, a Jacobite in 1745. [JA]

WRIGHT, JAMES, a weaver burgess of Arbroath, 1797. [AA. 18.941]
WRIGHT, JOHN, a glover in Arbroath, 1730s. [AER.95]
WRIGHT, JON., in Gallowden, Arbroath, 1752. [AER]
WRIGHT, JON., the younger, in Gallowden, Arbroath, 1752. [AER]
WYLLIE, JEAN, daughter of John Wyllie and Isobel Hamilton sister of Thomas Hamilton, joint heir to the said Thomas Hamilton a bailie of Arbroath, 1686. [NAS.Retours.Forfar]
WYLLIE, MARGARET, daughter of John Wyllie and Isobel Hamilton sister of Thomas Hamilton, joint heir to the said Thomas Hamilton a bailie of Arbroath, 1686. [NAS.Retours.Forfar]
WYLLIE, THOMAS, a burgess of Arbroath, 1682; hearth tax, St Vigeans, 1691. [NAS.E69.11.1][ACB]
WYLLIE, THOMAS, hearth tax, Arbroath, 1691. [NAS.E69.11.1]
YEAMAN, JEAN, hearth tax, Arbirlot, 1691. [NAS.E69.11.1]
YOUNG, GEORGE, a haydresser burgess of Arbroath, 1797. [AA.18.941]
YOUNG, Sir PETER, of Seaton, born 1543, tutor to King James VI, died 1628. [St Vigeans MI]
YEAMAN, PATRICK, landowner of Peebles, 1770. [DLS.26]
YOUNG, ROBERT, a weaver burgess of Arbroath, 1799. [AA.18.941]

www.ingramcontent.com/pod-product-compliance
Lightning Source LLC
Chambersburg PA
CBHW070513090426
42735CB00012B/2761